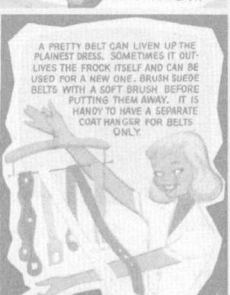

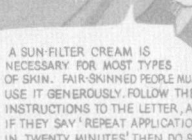

CHARM SCHOOL

This is a Prion Book

First published in the UK in 2007 by Prion
An imprint of the Carlton Publishing Group
20 Mortimer Street
London W1T 3JW

Pubished under licence from DC Comics

ISBN: 978-1-85375-617-7

The publishers would like to thank David Abbott at IPC for all his help in
compiling this book.

Edited and compiled by Lara Maiklem

Senior Art Editor: Gülen Shevki Taylor
Design: Tim Pattinson
Production: Janette Burgin

Concerning YOU

The Art of SOCIAL POISE

THAT ELUSIVE QUALITY CALLED 'POISE' OFTEN TAKES YEARS TO LEARN. BUT HERE ARE A FEW TRICKS WHICH WILL HELP YOU TO AVOID AWKWARD MOMENTS.

YOUR FIRST SAFEGUARD IS TO DRESS SUITABLY AND CAREFULLY. NOTHING MAKES ONE FEEL CLUMSIER THAN HAVING TO FIDGET WITH A COLLAR OR TRYING TO TUCK IN A BLOUSE.

PEOPLE TEND TO FIDGET WHEN THEY ARE NERVOUS. YOU CAN HELP YOURSELF RELAX BY SITTING DOWN GRACEFULLY AND COMFORTABLY. LET YOUR HANDS LIE TOGETHER, PALMS UPWARDS IN YOUR LAP.

SOME PEOPLE FIND IT DIFFICULT TO WALK ACROSS A ROOM WITHOUT KNOCKING INTO THINGS. IF THIS IS YOUR PROBLEM WHY NOT SET UP AN OBSTACLE COURSE AT HOME, AND PRACTISE ON IT?

ALWAYS CONCENTRATE ON THE PERSON WHO IS TALKING TO YOU. YOU WILL LOOK RESTLESS AND UNEASY IF YOU LET YOUR EYES ROAM AROUND THE ROOM. DON'T GO TO THE OPPOSITE EXTREME, HOWEVER, AND TRANSFIX THEM WITH A STEADY GLARE!

IF YOU HAVE TO PUT DOWN YOUR GLOVES AND OTHER BELONGINGS, DO PUT THEM SOMEWHERE ACCESSIBLE. IT SAVES TROUBLE FOR EVERYONE!

Contents

INTRODUCTION 6

1. HOW TO MAKE THE VERY BEST OF YOURSELF 8

2. I WANT TO BE...: ESSENTIAL CAREERS ADVICE FOR THE MODERN GIRL 22

3. CONCERNING YOU: CORRECT BEHAVIOUR FOR EVERY SITUATION 78

INTRODUCTION

Welcome to 1950s Britain, where the main things concerning any 'decent' girl included how to behave on a country visit, put together a delightful flower arrangement and follow a chosen career as a missionary.

Launched in 1951 as 'the New Super Colour Weekly for Every Girl', *Girl* provided a wealth of inspirational features, adventure stories, beauty and fashion tips, advice and, of course, pin-ups for half a million teenage girls throughout the fifties. Each week, strips like 'Charm School', 'I Want To Be' and 'Concerning You' offered no-nonsense, practical advice – all delivered with cut-glass grammar.

While 'Charm School' and 'Concerning You' gave invaluable advice on hair, beauty, clothes, socializing, hobbies, exercise, frugal habits and appropriate behaviour, 'I Want To Be' appealed to girls with their sights set firmly above the kitchen sink. For the career-minded girl it provided invaluable information on a range of careers, from the predictable (nanny, hairdresser and shop assistant) to the ambitious (doctor, barrister and chartered accountant) and downright bizarre (plastics designer, teacher of the blind and club leader). Required qualifications, training and expected salaries could be found, and most strips even managed to highlight the added benefit of being able to socialize with some really smashing chaps.

How things have changed since your mother, or grandmother, was joining her chums in a sewing circle… Surprisingly, however, many of the issues covered are common problems still blighting teenagers today – the difference being that the advice has a very distinct conservative twist.

For many, *Charm School* will be a nostalgic nod to the past that will bring memories flooding back; for others it will be a fascinating window on social history, a look back at a time when you counted yourself lucky to be taken on as a trainee accountant – 'a profession which is mainly open to men' – and straight stocking seams really did matter… a lot!

CHARM SCHOOL

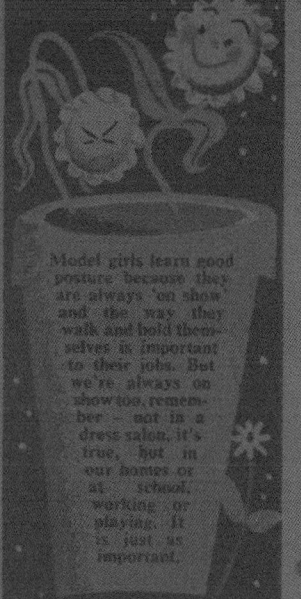

Model girls learn good posture because they are always 'on show' and the way they walk and hold themselves is important to their jobs. But we're always on show too, remember — not in a dress salon, it's true, but in our homes or at school, working or playing. It is just as important.

DON'T BE ASHAMED OF YOUR LOOKS — WALK AS IF YOU'RE PROUD OF THEM! BALANCING A BOOK ON YOUR HEAD WILL WORK WONDERS.

TRY NOT TO SLUMP OVER YOUR WORK, NOSE A FEW INCHES FROM IT. THIS IS BAD, NOT ONLY FOR YOUR LOOKS BUT FOR YOUR HEALTH TOO.

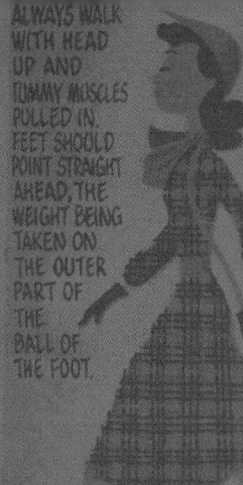

ALWAYS WALK WITH HEAD UP AND TUMMY MUSCLES PULLED IN. FEET SHOULD POINT STRAIGHT AHEAD, THE WEIGHT BEING TAKEN ON THE OUTER PART OF THE BALL OF THE FOOT.

REMEDY ROUND SHOULDERS BY STANDING, LEGS APART, BY CIRCLING ARMS BACKWARDS FROM SHOULDER.

— AND BY LYING DOWN FLAT AND MOVING YOUR ARMS IN A HALF-CIRCLE OVER YOUR HEAD.

CIRCLING YOUR LEGS (ONE AT A TIME) FROM THE THIGH EVERY MORNING AND EVENING WILL HELP TO GET RID OF THAT 'PUPPY' FAT.

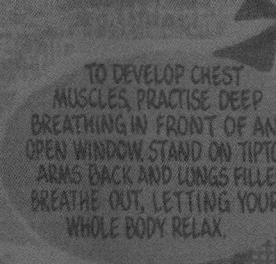

TO DEVELOP CHEST MUSCLES, PRACTISE DEEP BREATHING IN FRONT OF AN OPEN WINDOW. STAND ON TIPTOE, ARMS BACK AND LUNGS FILLED. BREATHE OUT, LETTING YOUR WHOLE BODY RELAX.

YOU WOULDN'T SIT LIKE ANY OF THE THREE GIRLS ABOVE, WOULD YOU? THE POSITION ON THE RIGHT IS THE CORRECT ONE, FEET NEATLY TOGETHER.

1

CHARM SCHOOL

How nice if we could all be like Tennyson's Rosebud *'sweet as English air could make her'*. But if we haven't a 'rosebud' complexion already, we can try to get one. For English girls, blessed already with a naturally good skin, a good complexion is mostly a matter of health and care. It is important for every girl to guard her health and take care of her natural beauty. In Charm School, you will learn how to do that. As 'your face is your fortune', we shall take that first, and describe here a different type of skin each week.

FIRST MEET CHRISTINE. (YOU MAY RECOGNISE YOUR OWN SKIN-TYPE IN HERS.) SHE'S A NICE LOOKING GIRL WITH GOOD REGULAR FEATURES. BUT OH, THOSE SPOTS! HER SKIN'S INCLINED TO BE GREASY AND, TRUE TO TYPE, SHE SUFFERS FROM DANDRUFF.

THE FIRST THING SHE SHOULD DO IS ASK HER MOTHER TO HELP BY GIVING HER PLENTY OF THE FOODS SHOWN IN THIS BASKET. (DANDRUFF SHOWS THAT THERE IS A DEFICIENCY IN HER DIET.)

SHE CAN TACKLE THE DANDRUFF WITH MEDICATED SHAMPOO (QUITE CHEAP AND IT LASTS SEVERAL TIMES). SHE SHOULD LATHER TWICE AND RINSE UNTIL HER HAIR 'SQUEAKS'. TO DRY IT SHE SHOULD USE A HUCKABACK, RATHER THAN A TURKISH TOWEL.

SKINS LIKE CHRISTINE'S CAN STAND LOTS OF SOAP, PREFERABLY WITH A COAL TAR BASE. SHE MUST *NEVER* PRESS BLACKHEADS, BUT GET RID OF THEM BY TAKING TWO SULPHUR TABLETS A DAY AND PLENTY OF EXERCISE IN FRESH AIR.

SHE SHOULD USE EAU DE COLOGNE ON COTTON-WOOL ONCE A MONTH (NOT MORE!) TO WIPE FACE AND NECK. AN ASTRINGENT IS USEFUL AFTER A COLD RINSE WHEN WASHING; USE WITCH-HAZEL OR ASK A CHEMIST TO MAKE ONE UP FROM ONE-PART FRIAR'S BALSAM TO TWENTY PARTS ROSEWATER.

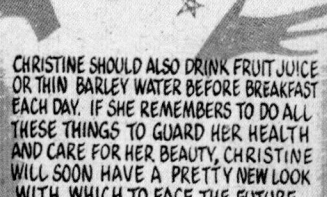

CHRISTINE SHOULD ALSO DRINK FRUIT JUICE OR THIN BARLEY WATER BEFORE BREAKFAST EACH DAY. IF SHE REMEMBERS TO DO ALL THESE THINGS TO GUARD HER HEALTH AND CARE FOR HER BEAUTY, CHRISTINE WILL SOON HAVE A PRETTY NEW LOOK WITH WHICH TO FACE THE FUTURE.

CHARM SCHOOL

Daphne's skin, in the words of the weather reports, is 'fine and dry' — the exact opposite of the greasy skin we talked about last week. This skin is most often found among girls with fair or bronze hair. Properly cared for it can look very lovely but it is inclined to flake and crack, especially in the winter.

DRY SKIN IS DAPHNE'S BIG PROBLEM. IF SHE'S WISE SHE'LL ALWAYS USE SUPER-FATTED SOAP AND, IN VERY COLD WEATHER, CLEANSING MILK ON A PAD OF COTTON-WOOL INSTEAD OF WASHING.

HER LIPS ARE OFTEN CRACKED AND PAINFUL SO SHE SHOULD RUB IN CAMPHOR ICE LAST THING AT NIGHT AND BEFORE SHE GOES OUT.

DAPHNE'S DIET CAN WORK WONDERS WITH HER SKIN — IT SHOULD INCLUDE COD-LIVER OIL CAPSULES, CITRUS FRUITS AND AS MUCH BUTTER AS POSSIBLE.

VANISHING CREAM USED DURING THE DAY WILL STOP CHAPPING AND WIND-BURN. AT NIGHT, BECAUSE HER SKIN IS INCLINED TO FLAKE AND WRINKLE, DAPHNE SHOULD ASK HER MOTHER FOR A LITTLE NOURISHING SKIN FOOD.

DRY HAIR IS ANOTHER OF DAPHNE'S PROBLEMS BUT SHE CAN TACKLE THIS BY USING A LANOLINE SHAMPOO WEEKLY AND A SPECIAL OIL SHAMPOO ONCE A MONTH.

A RECONDITIONING CREAM WILL PUT THE NATURAL OILS BACK INTO HER HAIR —

—AND DAPHNE WILL BE ABLE TO FACE THE FUTURE WITHOUT A CARE IN THE WORLD!

CHARM SCHOOL

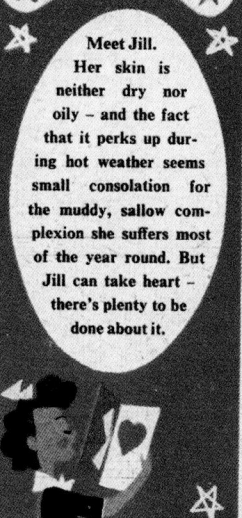

Meet Jill. Her skin is neither dry nor oily – and the fact that it perks up during hot weather seems small consolation for the muddy, sallow complexion she suffers most of the year round. But Jill can take heart – there's plenty to be done about it.

BLOCKED UP PORES ARE JILL'S WORRY SO SHE SHOULD AVOID USING TOO MUCH SOAP AND PAY MORE ATTENTION TO RINSING THAN WASHING. THREE RINSES IN HOT WATER AND THREE IN COLD AREN'T TOO MANY.

JILL'S SKIN BRIGHTENS UP IN SUMMER BECAUSE OF THE EXTRA VITAMIN D (THE SUNSHINE VITAMIN). IN WINTER SHE SHOULD GO OUT WALKING AS MUCH AS POSSIBLE.

HER COMPLEXION NEEDS STIMULATING WITH A LOOFAH OR COMPLEXION BRUSH BOTH IN THE BATH AND DURING MORNING AND EVENING WASHES.

SHE SHOULD APPLY SOAP SPARINGLY TO THE BRUSH AND SCRUB HER FACE GENTLY IN SMALL CIRCLES. RINSING *MUST* BE THOROUGH.

PATTING IN GLYCERINE AND ROSEWATER NIGHTLY WILL HELP TO KEEP HER SKIN SOFT AND GLOWING.

FRESH AIR, A STRICT EYE ON INNER CLEANLINESS, PLENTY OF SALADS, GREENS, FRUIT AND MILK AND JILL'S MUDDY LOOK WILL SOON BE A THING OF THE PAST.

CHARM SCHOOL

Just as there is more than one type of skin, so there are many types of hair. But whatever your type may be, remember that a weekly shampoo is the first step towards hair care and beauty — for it's cleanliness that counts in the long run.

CHRISTINE IS A WISE GIRL— SHE KNOWS THAT HAIR-BRUSHES SHOULD BE WASHED WEEKLY, COMBS EVERY OTHER DAY AT LEAST.

LANK AND DRY? THEN USE A LANOLINE SHAMPOO FOR A FEW WEEKS TO NOURISH THE ROOTS.

IF CHRISTINE'S HAIR IS UNRULY AFTER WASHING SHE SHOULD SPRAY IT WITH BRILLIANTINE. TOO MUCH LOOKS AWFUL— THE RIGHT AMOUNT MAKES ALL THE DIFFERENCE.

A PIECE OF SOFT SOAP DISSOLVED IN HOT WATER MAKES A GOOD SHAMPOO. AND HALF A PINT OF BOILING WATER POURED OVER A HANDFUL OF ROSEMARY LEAVES MAKES A FRAGRANT RINSE AFTER IT HAS BEEN COOLED AND STRAINED.

GIRLS WITH OVAL FACES SHOULD SAY NO TO A HARD UNBECOMING HAIR STYLE LIKE THIS.

CHRISTINE KNOWS THAT A WELL-BRUSHED, SIMPLE STYLE SUITS HER SMALL 'CHEEKY' FEATURES.

IF YOUR FACE IS PLUMP, AVOID FRINGES WHICH TEND TO GIVE A SQUARE LOOK.

CURLS ARE ATTRACTIVE BUT BEWARE OF THAT FUZZY-WUZZY LOOK! STEEL CURLERS TEND TO SPLIT THE HAIR SO USE THE SOFT PIPE-CLEANER TYPE INSTEAD.

REGULAR BRUSHING, REGULAR WASHING, THOROUGH RINSING IN LOTS OF WARM WATER —— AND CHRISTINE WON'T HAVE A HAIR CARE IN THE WORLD!

CHARM SCHOOL

Hands play a very important part in every girl's plan for good looks, for they are always on show. But don't give up in despair if you have not been blessed with beautiful hands – and don't try to hide them! Instead, make an effort to right matters straight away.

DAPHNE'S WORRY IS HER HANDS. BECAUSE THEY'RE NOT AS SLENDER AND SUPPLE AS SHE'D LIKE, SHE SHOULD PRACTISE FIVE FINGER EXERCISES IN A BOWL OF SOAPY WATER AND USE A NAILBRUSH VIGOROUSLY.

ANOTHER OF DAPHNE'S WORRIES—SPLITTING NAILS—WILL SOON VANISH IF SHE FILES THEM INSTEAD OF CUTTING THEM. SHE IS ALSO LEARNING TO GIVE HERSELF A WEEKLY 'PROFESSIONAL' MANICURE. THERE ARE FIVE STEPS AND IT ISN'T NEARLY AS DIFFICULT AS IT SOUNDS!

FIRST OF ALL, DAPHNE SOAKS HER HANDS IN WARM WATER FOR FIVE MINUTES AND THEN SCRUBS THE NAILS.

NEXT SHE RUNS THE POINTED END OF AN ORANGE STICK BENEATH EACH FINGER TIP AND USES A MANICURE PENCIL UNDER HER NAILS TO MAKE THEM LOOK WHITER.

WITH THE OTHER END OF THE ORANGE STICK TIPPED BY A SMALL PIECE OF COTTON-WOOL, DAPHNE PRESSES DOWN THE CUTICLES.

THEN SHE BUFFS HER NAILS WELL WITH SHORT, SHARP STROKES TO GIVE THEM A SHINE.

LASTLY, DAPHNE BORROWS A LITTLE HAND-CREAM FROM HER MOTHER AND SMOOTHES IT WELL IN WITH HER FINGERS.

AFTER THIS TREATMENT DAPHNE'S HANDS CAN BE ON SHOW FOR EVERYONE TO SEE!

CHARM SCHOOL

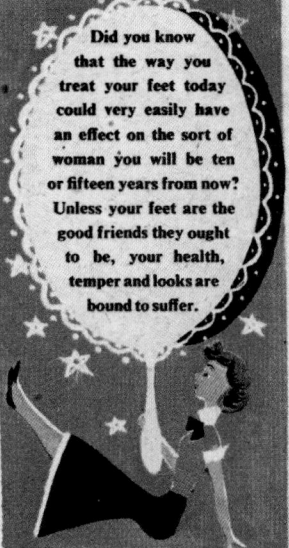

Did you know that the way you treat your feet today could very easily have an effect on the sort of woman you will be ten or fifteen years from now? Unless your feet are the good friends they ought to be, your health, temper and looks are bound to suffer.

JILL KNOWS HOW IMPORTANT IT IS TO TAKE GOOD CARE OF HER FEET SO SHE WASHES THEM DAILY AND SPRINKLES TALCUM BETWEEN HER TOES

TO STRENGTHEN HER ARCHES, JILL STANDS FOR A SECOND OR TWO ON THE OUTER EDGES OF HER FEET

IN WINTER-TIME JILL SHOULD BUY STOCKINGS OR SOCKS THAT ARE HALF AN INCH LONGER THAN HER BIG TOE.

WHEN HER LEGS AND FEET ARE DRY OR SCALY, JILL MASSAGES THEM WITH LANOLINE EVERY DAY.

BECAUSE HER FEET ARE A LITTLE FLAT, JILL SHOULD WALK AROUND THE ROOM ON TIP-TOE AS MUCH AS POSSIBLE. SHE SHOULD ALSO CURL AND UNCURL HER TOES WHEN SITTING DOWN.

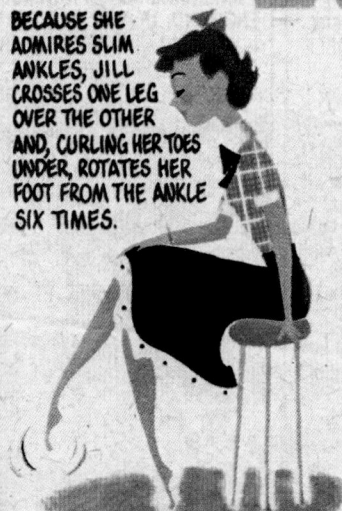

BECAUSE SHE ADMIRES SLIM ANKLES, JILL CROSSES ONE LEG OVER THE OTHER AND, CURLING HER TOES UNDER, ROTATES HER FOOT FROM THE ANKLE SIX TIMES.

JILL HAS LEARNT TO BUY SHOES THAT FIT SNUGLY ROUND THE HEEL YET LEAVE ROOM FOR HER TOES TO MOVE FREELY— SHE ALWAYS KEEPS THEM IN GOOD SHAPE WITH SHOE TREES.

CHARM SCHOOL

The good looks we all long to possess depend not so much on classic features as on good health. And in just the same way good health depends on good habits – habits which, formed when we are young, will safeguard our looks and our health for the rest of our life.

CLEANLINESS IS AS IMPORTANT *INSIDE* AS OUT — SO DRINK PLENTY OF WATER AND FRUIT JUICE,

SLEEP WITH YOUR WINDOW OPEN. THE IDEA THAT NIGHT AIR IS HARMFUL WENT OUT WITH CRINOLINES!

BUT THE NOTION OUR GRANDMOTHERS HAD ABOUT BRUSHING THEIR HAIR A HUNDRED TIMES AT NIGHT WAS A JOLLY GOOD ONE. PLEASE COPY.

CLEAN YOUR TEETH TWICE DAILY AT LEAST. IF YOU WANT TO GIVE THEM A PARTY SPARKLE, DIP YOUR BRUSH IN BICARBONATE OF SODA AND FINISH OFF WITH THAT.

TRY TO GET OUT INTO THE FRESH AIR AT LEAST ONCE A DAY. PRACTISE DEEP BREATHING AS YOU WALK TO SCHOOL— AND PRACTISE THRIFT WITH ALL THE BUS FARES YOU SAVE!

EAT LOTS OF FRESH FRUIT AND VEGETABLES. A GRAND 'WAKE UP' DRINK IS THE JUICE OF ONE LEMON, SUGAR AND A FEW RAISINS STEEPED IN BOILING WATER. COVER AND LEAVE BY YOUR BED TO DRINK FIRST THING IN THE MORNING.

CHARM SCHOOL

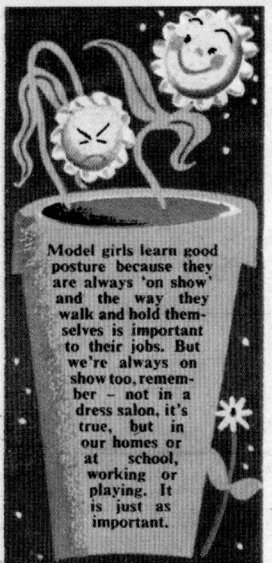

Model girls learn good posture because they are always 'on show' and the way they walk and hold themselves is important to their jobs. But we're always on show too, remember – not in a dress salon, it's true, but in our homes or at school, working or playing. It is just as important.

DON'T BE ASHAMED OF YOUR LOOKS— WALK AS IF YOU'RE PROUD OF THEM! BALANCING A BOOK ON YOUR HEAD WILL WORK WONDERS.

TRY NOT TO SLUMP OVER YOUR WORK, NOSE A FEW INCHES FROM IT. THIS IS BAD, NOT ONLY FOR YOUR LOOKS BUT FOR YOUR HEALTH TOO.

ALWAYS WALK WITH HEAD UP AND TUMMY MUSCLES PULLED IN. FEET SHOULD POINT STRAIGHT AHEAD, THE WEIGHT BEING TAKEN ON THE OUTER PART OF THE BALL OF THE FOOT.

REMEDY ROUND SHOULDERS BY STANDING, LEGS APART, AND CIRCLING **ARMS BACKWARDS FROM** SHOULDER.

—AND BY LYING DOWN FLAT AND MOVING YOUR ARMS IN A HALF-CIRCLE OVER YOUR HEAD.

CIRCLING YOUR LEGS (ONE AT A TIME) FROM THE THIGH EVERY MORNING AND EVENING WILL HELP TO GET RID OF THAT 'PUPPY' FAT.

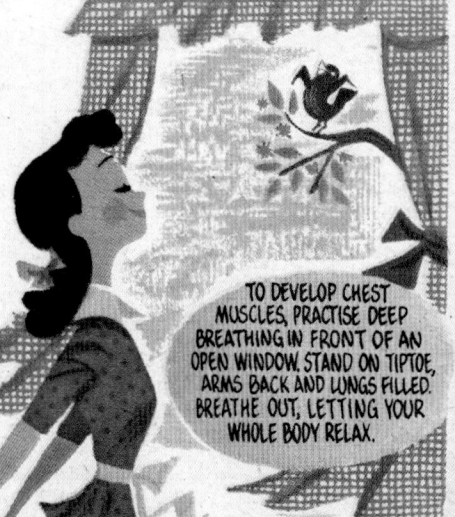

TO DEVELOP CHEST MUSCLES, PRACTISE DEEP BREATHING IN FRONT OF AN OPEN WINDOW. STAND ON TIPTOE, ARMS BACK AND LUNGS FILLED. BREATHE OUT, LETTING YOUR WHOLE BODY RELAX.

YOU WOULDN'T SIT LIKE ANY OF THE THREE GIRLS ABOVE, WOULD YOU? THE POSITION ON THE RIGHT IS THE CORRECT ONE, FEET NEATLY TOGETHER.

CHARM SCHOOL

Potter.G

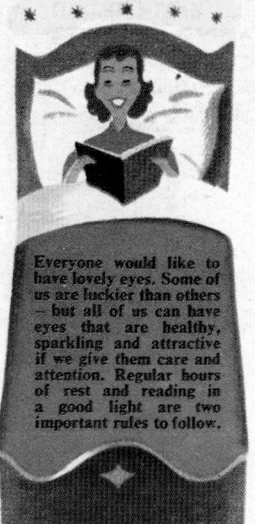

Everyone would like to have lovely eyes. Some of us are luckier than others — but all of us can have eyes that are healthy, sparkling and attractive if we give them care and attention. Regular hours of rest and reading in a good light are two important rules to follow.

PREVENT EYE STRAIN BY READING AND WRITING IN A GOOD LIGHT. IT SHOULD COME, PREFERABLY, FROM BEHIND YOUR LEFT SHOULDER.

A DAILY EYE-BATH IS A VERY GOOD HABIT AS IT WILL HELP TO KEEP YOUR EYES CLEAR AND SPARKLING. THE BEST TIME FOR IT IS IN THE EVENING.

IF YOU WEAR GLASSES THERE'S NO EXCUSE FOR THAT ROUND 'OWLISH' LOOK THESE DAYS.

THERE ARE ALL SORTS OF FRAMES TO CHOOSE FROM— SO MAKE SURE THE SHAPE SUITS YOUR FACE.

STRENGTHEN YOUR SIGHT BY STANDING AT AN OPEN WINDOW AND FOCUSING YOUR EYES ON A DISTANT OBJECT, THEN LOOKING SUDDENLY AT A NEAR ONE.

IF THERE'S A 'FOREIGN BODY' IN YOUR EYE, SLIP ON A BANDAGE AND GO TO A DOCTOR. IF YOU CANNOT GO AT ONCE A FEW DROPS OF CASTOR OIL MAY FLOAT THE OBJECT OUT

EYELASHES WILL GROW IF YOU BRUSH THEM DAILY WITH OLIVE OIL. BUT ALWAYS BRUSH UPWARDS.

CHARM SCHOOL

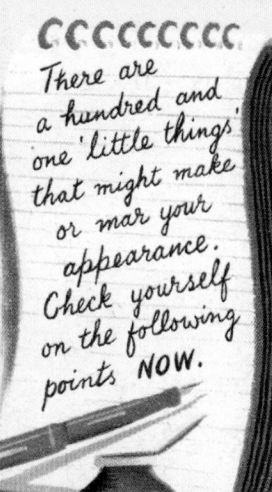

There are a hundred and one 'little things' that might make or mar your appearance. Check yourself on the following points NOW.

HAVE YOU EVER WALKED BEHIND ANYONE WHOSE STOCKING SEAMS LOOKED LIKE WAVY TRAMLINES? MAKE SURE YOURS NEVER DO!

IN GRANDMA'S DAY IT WAS SAID YOU COULD ALWAYS TELL A LADY BY HER CLEAN HANDKERCHIEF. THAT'S WORTH REMEMBERING TODAY AS WELL.

OF COURSE YOU'LL TAKE YOUR SHOES TO BE REPAIRED LONG BEFORE THEY LOOK LIKE THIS, WON'T YOU?

GIVE YOUR GLOVES A REGULAR CHECK OVER FOR SPLIT SEAMS AND NEVER WEAR LIGHT-COLOURED ONES THAT ARE SOILED.

LAUNDER WASH-LEATHER GLOVES ON YOUR HANDS. RINSE WELL BUT FINALLY LATHER WITH SOAP, WATER AND A FEW DROPS OF OLIVE OIL. DRY WITHOUT RINSING AGAIN.

COAT HANGERS WILL LENGTHEN THE LIFE OF ALL YOUR CLOTHES AS WELL AS PREVENTING UGLY CREASES.

CHARM SCHOOL

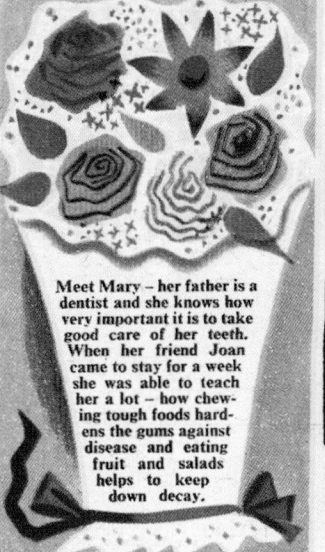

Meet Mary – her father is a dentist and she knows how very important it is to take good care of her teeth. When her friend Joan came to stay for a week she was able to teach her a lot – how chewing tough foods hardens the gums against disease and eating fruit and salads helps to keep down decay.

MARY AND HER FATHER TOOK JOAN ON A VISIT TO THE ZOO.

MARY'S FATHER TOLD JOAN: "LOOK AT THE LION'S TEETH — THEY'RE STRONG AND HEALTHY BECAUSE HE CHEWS BONES AND EATS RAW MEAT. HE WORKS HIS TEETH HARD AND THAT MAKES THEM HEALTHY."

HE EXPLAINED THAT ESKIMOS ALSO HAVE PERFECT TEETH BECAUSE THEY SOFTEN UP HIDES WITH THEM AND NEVER EAT SWEET, STICKY FOODS WHICH CAUSE DECAY.

BACK HOME FOR TEA — AND JOAN LEARNT THAT SHE COULD STILL ENJOY SWEET THINGS ONLY SHE *MUST* FINISH THE MEAL WITH ONE OF THE CLEANSING FOODS LIKE —

— SALAD, CELERY, CARROTS, LETTUCE, APPLES OR NUTS. THESE FOODS CLEAN AWAY THE SWEET PARTICLES WHICH GET BETWEEN THE TEETH AND START DECAY ALMOST AT ONCE.

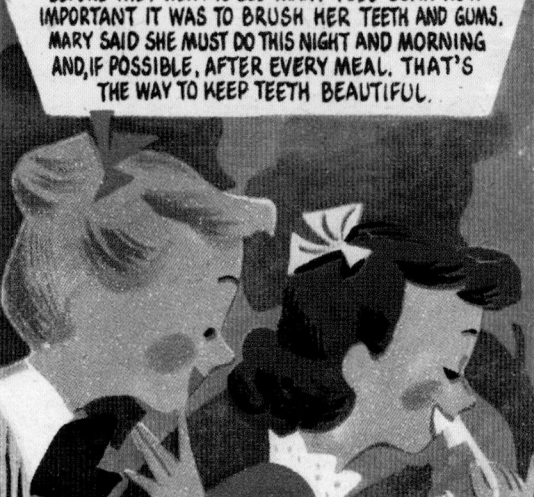

BEFORE THEY WENT TO BED MARY TOLD JOAN HOW IMPORTANT IT WAS TO BRUSH HER TEETH AND GUMS. MARY SAID SHE MUST DO THIS NIGHT AND MORNING AND, IF POSSIBLE, AFTER EVERY MEAL. THAT'S THE WAY TO KEEP TEETH BEAUTIFUL.

CHARM SCHOOL

Here are Mary and her friend Joan, who is staying with her. Mary's father is a dentist, so last week she was able to tell Joan about all the things that help to make teeth healthy and attractive. This week she teaches her a lot more about how to *keep* her teeth that way.

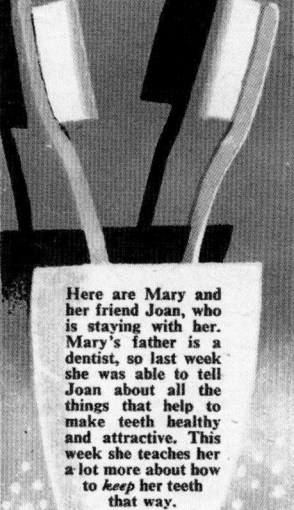

USE ABOUT AN INCH, THAT'S ALL — IT'S THE BRUSHING THAT COUNTS.

MARY TOLD JOAN HOW IMPORTANT IT IS TO CHOOSE A GOOD TOOTHPASTE.

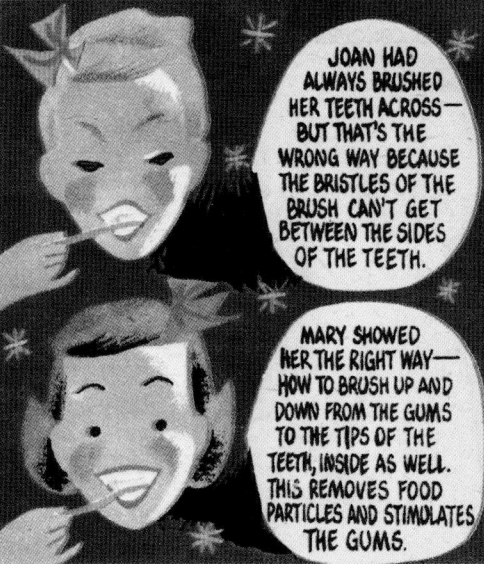

JOAN HAD ALWAYS BRUSHED HER TEETH ACROSS — BUT THAT'S THE WRONG WAY BECAUSE THE BRISTLES OF THE BRUSH CAN'T GET BETWEEN THE SIDES OF THE TEETH.

MARY SHOWED HER THE RIGHT WAY — HOW TO BRUSH UP AND DOWN FROM THE GUMS TO THE TIPS OF THE TEETH, INSIDE AS WELL. THIS REMOVES FOOD PARTICLES AND STIMULATES THE GUMS.

IF THE BRISTLES OF YOUR BRUSH GET BROKEN LIKE JOAN'S, THEY CAN'T CLEAN THE TEETH PROPERLY. BUY A NEW ONE.

WHEN JOAN HAD TOOTHACHE BECAUSE ONE OF HER TEETH NEEDED FILLING, MARY PERSUADED HER TO GO TO THE DENTIST AT ONCE.

IT DIDN'T HURT AT ALL BECAUSE MARY'S FATHER GAVE JOAN AN INJECTION. MORE IMPORTANT STILL, THE TOOTH WAS SAVED.

JOAN LEARNT A LOT ABOUT HER MOUTH FROM MARY AND SHE'S GOING TO PUT IT ALL INTO PRACTICE — PARTICULARLY THE BIT ABOUT SEEING A DENTIST EVERY SIX MONTHS!

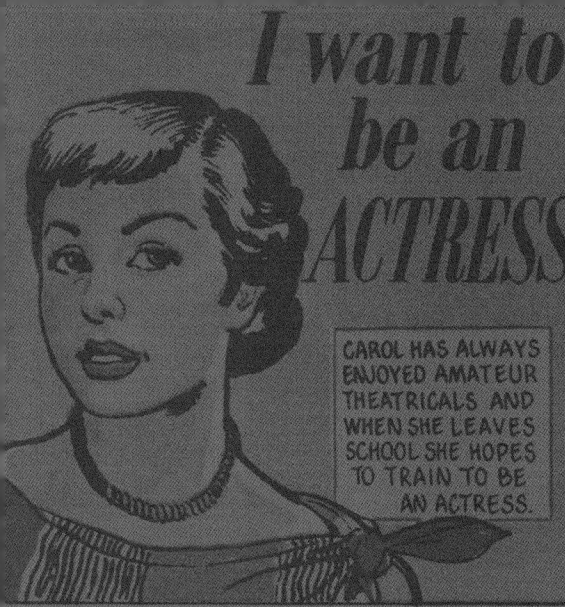

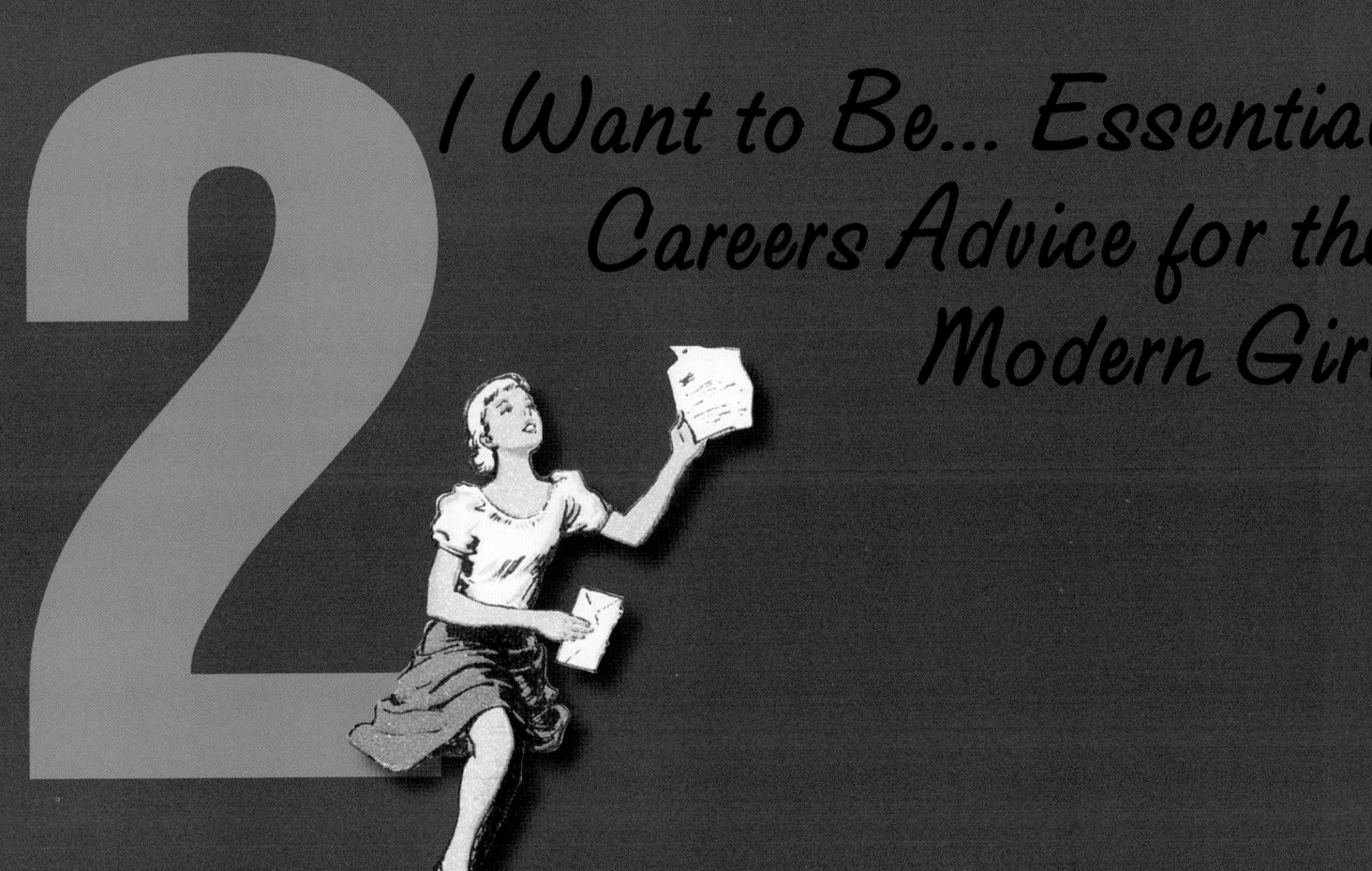

2

I Want to Be... Essential Careers Advice for the Modern Girl

I want to be a NURSE

Molly Jones has been accepted as a student nurse at a large hospital. She had to produce a medical and dental certificate and have reached a good standard of education. She has been interviewed by the Matron, who approves of her, and begins her career with three months at the Preliminary Training School.

I HOPE YOU WILL BE HAPPY WITH US, NURSE JONES. YOU'LL FIND THERE'S A LOT TO LEARN.

THANK YOU, SISTER, I'M SURE I SHALL.

HAVING PASSED HER P.T.S. EXAM, MOLLY HAS BEGUN HER FIRST JOB IN THE HOSPITAL PROPER AS A JUNIOR STUDENT NURSE ON THE MALE SURGICAL WARD. SHE CARES FOR THE HYGIENE OF THE PATIENTS AND WILL, AS SHE BECOMES MORE SKILLED, PREPARE THEM FOR OPERATIONS AND DO SIMPLE DRESSINGS.

NOW IN HER SECOND YEAR, MOLLY ATTENDS LECTURES AND HAS PASSED HER FIRST YEAR EXAM. SHE RECEIVES £225 A YEAR AND PAYS THE HOSPITAL £108 FOR BOARD AND LODGING. HER UNIFORM AND LAUNDRY ARE FREE.

NURSE JONES, CAN YOU TELL THE CLASS HOW MANY BONES THERE ARE IN THE HUMAN FOOT?

WILL YOU PASS ME THE FORCEPS PLEASE, NURSE.

IT'S MOLLY'S THIRD YEAR NOW AND SHE IS DOING PART OF HER TRAINING IN HOSPITAL DEPARTMENTS. SHE'S KEEN ON THE OPERATING THEATRE AND HOPES TO BE A STAFF NURSE THERE WHEN SHE HAS TAKEN HER FINAL EXAMS.

THIS IS A LOVELY CHANGE FROM BEING ON NIGHT DUTY!

YES, IT'S GREAT FUN, ISN'T IT.

HAVING FINISHED A PERIOD OF NIGHT DUTY ON THE CHILDREN'S WARD, MOLLY IS RELAXING AT ONE OF THE DANCES THE HOSPITAL FREQUENTLY HOLDS.

MOLLY, THRILLED AT ACHIEVING HER AMBITION, AT LAST RECEIVES HER CERTIFICATE FROM THE CHAIRMAN OF THE HOSPITAL.

THANK YOU VERY MUCH INDEED, SIR.

CONGRATULATIONS, NURSE. YOU'VE DONE WELL.

I want to be a KENNEL-MAID

Sue lives in the country and loves animals. There are some registered kennels near her home and when she leaves school she has arranged to be taken on there as a trainee kennelmaid.

COME ON, ROUGH, I'LL RACE YOU HOME FOR TEA!

SUE HAS HAD FIVE YEARS. SHE DISTEMPER AND BEHAVE IN TRAFFIC. HER DOG, ROUGH, FOR NURSED HIM THROUGH TAUGHT HIM HOW TO HER TRAINING OF HIM WILL BE VERY USEFUL IN HER NEW JOB.

YOU'LL FIND THAT HARD PAD IS VERY COMMON AMONG THIS BREED OF DOG...

SUE HAS BEEN AT THE KENNELS THREE MONTHS NOW. SHE ATTENDS LECTURES BY THE LOCAL VET, EXERCISES AND GROOMS THE DOGS AND LEARNS ABOUT THEIR DIETS.

HIS EARS NEED A LITTLE MORE ATTENTION, SUE.

SHE IS LEARNING HOW TO PREPARE DOGS FOR SHOWING UNDER THE INSTRUCTIONS OF THE MANAGERESS. SHE IS ALSO TAUGHT HOW TO RECORD PEDIGREES AND HAS ATTENDED THE LOCAL CANINE SURGERY TO WATCH OPERATIONS WHICH ARE, OF COURSE, CARRIED OUT ONLY BY FULLY QUALIFIED VETERINARY SURGEONS.

SUE'S FRIEND JUNE HAS FINISHED HER TRAINING AT THE KENNELS AND IS NOW A CANINE NURSE AT A VETERINARY HOSPITAL. HER WORK DEMANDS A HIGH DEGREE OF SKILL AND COMPETENCE.

The BERRY KENNELS (Reg)

I'M SO GLAD I TOOK THE TRAINING, DADDY.

NOW SUE AND HER FATHER OWN A SMALL KENNELS IN SUSSEX. AS WELL AS THE MANAGEMENT AND CARE OF DOGS, THEY BREED COCKER SPANIELS. IF YOU ARE A DOG LOVER YOU WILL FIND THE WORK OF A KENNELMAID BOTH VARIED AND SATISFYING.

I want to be a MODEL

MARY, WHO HAS JUST LEFT SCHOOL, IS PRETTY, SLENDER AND FIVE FEET FIVE INCHES TALL. HER AMBITION IS TO BE A MODEL.

SHE WANTS TO MODEL TEEN-AGE CLOTHES AND, REALISING THAT HER *OWN* APPEARANCE WILL BE IMPORTANT TO HER CAREER, SHE STUDIES FASHION MAGAZINES CAREFULLY TO LEARN ABOUT THE LATEST STYLES AND THE BEST WAYS TO WEAR THEM.

TIME TO STOP STUDYING, MARY—SUPPER'S READY!

I NEVER THOUGHT LEARNING TO WALK PROPERLY WAS SUCH HARD WORK.

MARY IS NOW TAKING A SIX WEEKS' COURSE AT A CHARM SCHOOL ATTACHED TO A MODEL AGENCY. SHE IS LEARNING THE BASIC MANNEQUIN MOVEMENTS, GENERAL DEPORTMENT, SOCIAL ETIQUETTE AND HOW TO USE MAKE-UP. THE COST OF THE COURSE IS ABOUT TWENTY GUINEAS.

THIS IS NOTHING. JUST WAIT UNTIL YOU BECOME A MANNEQUIN!

THE COURSE OVER, MARY POSES FOR A SELECTION OF STUDIO PHOTOGRAPHS. THESE, TOGETHER WITH A LIST OF HER MEASURE-MENTS, WILL BE KEPT BY THE MODEL AGENCY TO SHOW TO THEIR CLIENTS.

CHIN A LITTLE HIGHER, PLEASE.

I'LL LEAVE MY ADDRESS AND PHONE NUMBER.

YES— BUT WE MAY NOT HAVE ANY WORK FOR YOU FOR SOME WEEKS.

THE AGENCY WILL ARRANGE ENGAGE-MENTS FOR MARY. SHE KNOWS THERE MAY NOT BE MANY AT FIRST AND PLANS TO WORK PART-TIME IN THE DRESS SALON OF A LARGE STORE.

...AND THAT CONCLUDES OUR FASHION DISPLAY FOR THIS AFTER-NOON.

AFTER TWO YEARS MARY IS MODELLING REGULARLY AT DRESS SHOWS AND FOR FASHION PHOTOGRAPHERS. SHE EARNS ABOUT EIGHT POUNDS A WEEK. OUT OF THIS SHE HAS TO BUY ALL HER OWN ACCESS-ORIES AND MAKE-UP AND HAVE HER HAIR DONE REGULARLY, FOR SHE MUST *ALWAYS* LOOK IMMACULATE.

I want to be a Secretary

PAT CANNON LEAVES SCHOOL THIS TERM AND WANTS TO BE A SECRETARY. SHE HAS ENROLLED AT A LOCAL COMMERCIAL COLLEGE FOR A YEAR'S TRAINING IN SHORTHAND AND TYPING.

WILL YOU COME IN, MISS CANNON? I WANT TO DICTATE SOME LETTERS.

YES, MR ARMITAGE.

PAT HAS FINISHED HER YEAR'S TRAINING AND IS NOW A SHORTHAND TYPIST IN AN EXPORT FIRM. HER SALARY IS JUST OVER THREE POUNDS A WEEK AND SHE'S LEARNING A LOT ABOUT OFFICE ROUTINE.

PAT'S FIRM HAS BRANCHES IN FRANCE AND SPAIN, SO SHE IS LEARNING BOTH LANGUAGES AT NIGHT SCHOOL. THEY WILL BE USEFUL IF SHE EVER WANTS TO WORK ABROAD.

YOUR FRENCH SOUNDED PRETTY GOOD. TONIGHT, PAT.

THANKS, JOHN! SEE YOU ON THURSDAY.

SPANISH IS CERTAINLY A FLOWERY LANGUAGE, PAT.

IT'S A CHANGE FROM TYPING *DEAR SIR* ALL THE TIME!

AFTER TWO YEARS PAT HAS BECOME ONE OF TWO ASSISTANT SECRETARIES. SHE NOW EARNS ABOUT FIVE POUNDS A WEEK.

THERE WILL BE A VACANCY AT OUR HEAD OFFICE SOON. WOULD YOU LIKE IT?

OH YES, PLEASE!

HER EMPLOYERS ARE IMPRESSED BY PAT'S KEENNESS AND ABILITY. SHE IS ALWAYS WELL GROOMED, PUNCTUAL AND PLEASANT TO WORK WITH. NOW SHE HAS BEEN OFFERED THE POST OF PRIVATE SECRETARY TO THE CHIEF OF THE FIRM'S LONDON BRANCH.

PAT'S DREAMS HAVE ALL COME TRUE. SHE HAS AN INTERESTING, WELL-PAID JOB IN A BUSY PART OF LONDON AND KNOWS THAT HER HARD WORK AND TRAINING HAVE NOT BEEN WASTED.

I want to be a NANNY

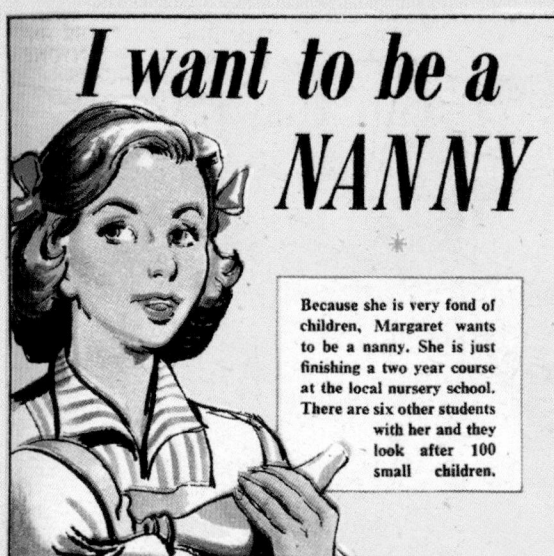

Because she is very fond of children, Margaret wants to be a nanny. She is just finishing a two year course at the local nursery school. There are six other students with her and they look after 100 small children.

MARGARET IS HELPING WITH HER LAST PARTY AT THE NURSERY BEFORE TAKING A JOB IN A PRIVATE HOUSE TO WORK UNDER A TRAINED NANNY. SHE WILL BE GIVEN A SALARY, FULL BOARD AND LODGING AND HAVE HER UNIFORM AND LAUNDRY BILLS PAID FOR HER.

...AND WE ALL FALL DOWN!

PASS ME THE SAFETY PINS PLEASE, MARGARET.

EXTREMELY HAPPY IN HER NEW JOB, MARGARET HELPS NANNY TO LOOK AFTER PAUL, AND FELICITY ANN WHO IS SIX MONTHS OLD. THERE ARE DAILY OUTINGS FOR BOTH OF THEM AND MARGARET LEARNS TO CARE FOR THEIR CLOTHES, DIETS AND HEALTH.

ARE WE NEARLY THERE, MARGARET?

MARGARET HAS BEEN IN HER JOB A YEAR NOW AND HER ANNUAL SALARY IS £110. HER EMPLOYER IS IN THE DIPLOMATIC SERVICE, SO SHE SOMETIMES TRAVELS ABROAD WITH THE FAMILY.

YES, PAUL. THERE IS THE SLOPE TO THE BEACH JUST AHEAD.

GOOD-BYE, FELICITY. I'LL BE HERE AGAIN AT LUNCHTIME.

FELICITY IS NOW FIVE AND GOES TO THE KINDERGARTEN EACH DAY. THERE IS LESS WORK TO DO IN THE NURSERY SO MARGARET HAS APPLIED FOR A NANNY'S POST ELSEWHERE.

MARGARET HAS STARTED HER NEW JOB AND HAS COMPLETE CHARGE OF YOUNG JONATHAN, WHO IS UNDER A YEAR OLD. SHE LOVES THE LIFE, SO IF *YOU'D* LIKE TO BE A NANNY YOU CAN TRAIN FOR IT AS SHE DID.

I want to be A RIDING TEACHER

VALERIE HAS HAD RIDING LESSONS SINCE SHE WAS QUITE SMALL. NOW SHE IS VERY KEEN TO BE AN INSTRUCTRESS WHEN SHE LEAVES SCHOOL.

THERE'S A VACANCY AT THE LOCAL RIDING SCHOOL AND VALERIE HAS GOT THE JOB. SHE WILL LEARN HOW TO CARE FOR THE HORSES AND WILL RECEIVE ONLY A SMALL SALARY FOR THE FIRST YEAR. THE AMOUNT VARIES IN DIFFERENT PARTS OF THE COUNTRY.

SHE HAS NOW BEEN AT THE SCHOOL FOR THREE YEARS AND HAS BEEN TAUGHT TO PREPARE AND RIDE HORSES FOR SHOW JUMPING. HER SALARY IS A HUNDRED AND FIFTY POUNDS A YEAR.

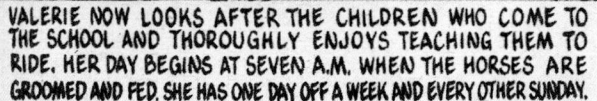

VALERIE NOW LOOKS AFTER THE CHILDREN WHO COME TO THE SCHOOL AND THOROUGHLY ENJOYS TEACHING THEM TO RIDE. HER DAY BEGINS AT SEVEN A.M. WHEN THE HORSES ARE GROOMED AND FED. SHE HAS ONE DAY OFF A WEEK AND EVERY OTHER SUNDAY.

AFTER SEVERAL YEARS OF INSTRUCTING, GROOMING AND GENERALLY CARING FOR THE HORSES AT THE SCHOOL, VALERIE HAS BECOME A FIRST CLASS HORSEWOMAN. AT THE LOCAL HORSE SHOW SHE HAS JUST WON A CUP FOR JUMPING.

VALERIE HAS BEEN TAKEN ON AS A PARTNER IN THE RIDING SCHOOL. SHE HAS LEARNT TO KNOW A GOOD HORSE AND HOW MUCH TO PAY FOR HIM — AND WOULDN'T CHANGE HER JOB FOR ANY OTHER IN THE WORLD!

I want to be a LIBRARIAN

BETTY HAS BEEN A BOOK-WORM EVER SINCE SHE COULD READ. SHE LEFT SCHOOL LAST TERM AFTER TAKING HER GENERAL SCHOOL CERTIFICATE AND HAS JOINED THE LOCAL LIBRARY AS A JUNIOR ASSISTANT.

IT'S TIME TO HAND IN YOUR PAPERS NOW, GIRLS!

BETTY HAS BEEN AT THE LIBRARY FOR A YEAR NOW AND IS TAKING HER FIRST EXAM. THIS COVERS THE CLASSIFICATION AND INDEXING OF BOOKS, A KNOWLEDGE OF ENGLISH LITERATURE AND REFERENCE METHODS.

ARE YOU ENJOYING IT, MOTHER?

YES — THOROUGHLY!

TO CELEBRATE PASSING THE EXAM, BETTY HAS TAKEN HER MOTHER TO THE BALLET. SHE NOW EARNS ABOUT THREE POUNDS A WEEK AND THIS AMOUNT WILL BE INCREASED EACH YEAR.

YES — AND I'M GLAD WE STAYED LATE TO ASK QUESTIONS.

THAT LECTURE TAUGHT ME A LOT, BETTY.

TWICE A WEEK BETTY GOES TO NIGHT SCHOOL WITH HER FRIEND JILL. THEY ARE BOTH STUDYING HARD SO THAT THEY CAN EVENTUALLY BE REGISTERED AS CHARTERED LIBRARIANS.

HAVING BEEN AT THE LIBRARY FIVE YEARS AND HAVING PASSED TWO MORE EXAMS, BETTY IS NOW A QUALIFIED LIBRARIAN. HER JOB IS PENSIONABLE AND SHE CAN EARN UP TO £600 A YEAR AS CHIEF OF A LIBRARY WHICH SERVES A LARGE TOWN.

NOW BETTY HAS TAKEN A JOB WITH AN IMPORTANT RESEARCH ORGANISATION. HER WORK INVOLVES DIGGING UP FACTS AND REMEMBERING THEM, CORRECT CLASSIFICATION OF THE THOUSANDS OF BOOKS IN HER CHARGE AND COMPILING UP-TO-DATE CATALOGUES. SHE LOVES IT!

LOVELY MORNING, MISS.

ISN'T IT? I'M TAKING MY LUNCH INTO THE PARK TODAY!

I want to be a BEAUTICIAN

Joyce leaves school this term. Interested in make-up, she has got a job at the beauty counter of a local store.

THIS CREAM IS JUST RIGHT FOR YOUR TYPE OF SKIN, MADAM.

ALL RIGHT THEN—I'LL TRY IT!

SHE HAS BEEN AT THE STORE FOR TWELVE MONTHS NOW AND IS QUICKLY LEARNING HER JOB. AFTER ANOTHER SIX MONTHS HER FATHER IS PAYING FOR HER TO DO A YEAR'S TRAINING AT A BEAUTY SCHOOL IN LONDON.

I THINK I'M GETTING THE IDEA NOW.

YES, THAT'S BETTER. YOU MUST ALWAYS MASSAGE LIGHTLY AND GENTLY.

AT THE SCHOOL THE STUDENTS PRACTISE ON ONE ANOTHER. JOYCE IS AT PRESENT LEARNING ABOUT FACE MASSAGE, BUT THE FULL COURSE DEALS WITH EVERY TYPE OF BEAUTY PROBLEM.

GOOD-BYE, MISS EDWARDS, AND THANK YOU FOR ALL YOU'VE DONE.

GOOD-BYE, MY DEAR. REMEMBER WHAT WE'VE TAUGHT YOU!

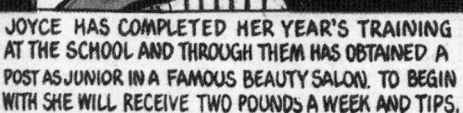

JOYCE HAS COMPLETED HER YEAR'S TRAINING AT THE SCHOOL AND THROUGH THEM HAS OBTAINED A POST AS JUNIOR IN A FAMOUS BEAUTY SALON. TO BEGIN WITH SHE WILL RECEIVE TWO POUNDS A WEEK AND TIPS.

ARE YOU PLEASED WITH THE RESULTS OF THE TREATMENT?

YES. I'LL MAKE ANOTHER APPOINTMENT FOR NEXT WEEK.

JOYCE WILL BE FREE IN FIVE MINUTES, MADAM.

AT THE SALON JOYCE'S COURTESY AND CONSIDERATION HAVE WON HER MANY CLIENTS WHO ASK SPECIALLY FOR HER. SHE IS VERY HAPPY THERE AND NOW EARNS FIVE POUNDS A WEEK.

JUST WATCH HOW SMOOTHLY THIS LIPSTICK GOES ON.

JOYCE IS NOW GETTING MORE EXPERIENCE BY TRAVELLING ROUND THE COUNTRY DEMONSTRATING THE BEAUTY PRODUCTS OF A WELL-KNOWN LONDON FIRM. BESIDES HER SALARY SHE GETS A TRAVELLING ALLOWANCE AND COMMISSION ON THE PRODUCTS SHE SELLS.

I want to be a HOTEL RECEPTIONIST

*

DIANA IS VERY KEEN ON MEETING PEOPLE AND FOR TWO YEARS NOW, EVER SINCE SHE LEFT SCHOOL, HAS BEEN ASSISTANT RECEPTIONIST IN A LARGE HOTEL

SHE CONSULTS MRS SIMS, THE HOUSEKEEPER, ABOUT THE NUMBER OF EMPTY ROOMS. SOME MAY BE 'OFF' FOR SPRING-CLEANING AND DIANA HAS TO SEE THAT THE HOTEL IS NEITHER UNDER NOR OVER- BOOKED.

HOW LONG WILL IT TAKE TO SPRING-CLEAN THOSE TWO ROOMS, MRS SIMS?

OH, NOT MORE THAN A WEEK, MISS.

TRÈS BIEN, MONSIEUR.

DIANA ALSO HAS TO DEAL WITH MANY FOREIGN VISITORS AND THE FRENCH SHE LEARNED AT NIGHT SCHOOL IS A GREAT ASSET TO HER. HER SALARY IS ABOUT THREE POUNDS A WEEK, PLUS FREE BOARD AND LODGING, AND IT WILL BE INCREASED GRADUALLY.

DO YOU MIND DOING AN EXTRA HOUR'S DUTY FOR ME TODAY, JOAN?

NOT A BIT, DIANA. I'LL SEE YOU AT SIX INSTEAD OF FIVE THEN.

AFTER FOUR YEARS DIANA IS NOW SENIOR RECEPTIONIST AND HAS HER MEALS WITH THE OTHER SENIOR MEMBERS OF THE HOTEL STAFF. SHE SHARES HER DUTIES WITH THE OTHER RECEPTIONIST.

WE'RE DELIGHTED TO SEE YOU AGAIN, SIR.

THANK YOU. IT'S NICE TO BE BACK!

MAKING A LIST OF REGULAR VISITORS TO THE HOTEL AND REMEMBERING THEIR LIKES AND DISLIKES IS ONE OF DIANA'S MAIN DUTIES. SHE HAS BEEN IN HER JOB TEN YEARS NOW AND HER SMARTNESS, EFFICIENCY AND GOOD MANNERS HAVE MADE HER A GREAT FAVOURITE WITH THE GUESTS.

DIANA IS DRESSING FOR THE ANNUAL STAFF BALL HELD AT THE HOTEL. SHE IS VERY HAPPY IN HER JOB — NOT ONLY BECAUSE SHE LIKES THE WORK BUT BECAUSE SHE HAS MADE MANY FIRM FRIENDS.

I want to be an AIR STEWARDESS

PAULINE wants to be an air stewardess and, although she knows how difficult it is, has made a good start by passing her general certificate with a distinction in French.

DOES THAT FEEL MORE COMFORTABLE, MRS SAUVEY?

MUCH BETTER, NURSE.

A MEMBER OF THE RED CROSS, PAULINE IS DOING FULL-TIME WORK IN HER LOCAL HOSPITAL. AIR STEWARDESSES NEED TO KNOW HOW TO CARE FOR SICK PASSENGERS AND PAULINE WILL DO TWO YEARS NURSING TO HELP REALISE HER CHERISHED AMBITION.

I DO HOPE MY APPLICATION HAS BEEN SUCCESSFUL.

WE'LL LET YOU KNOW OUR DECISION IN A FEW DAYS, MISS NICHOLS.

PAULINE'S GREAT DAY HAS ARRIVED AND SHE HAS BEEN GRANTED AN INTERVIEW WITH THE AIRLINE AUTHORITIES. SHE IS NOW TWENTY-ONE, WITH A SOUND KNOWLEDGE OF NURSING AND FRENCH. TOGETHER WITH HER FRIENDLY PERSONALITY AND GOOD GROOMING SHE HOPES HER APPLICATION WILL BE SUCCESSFUL.

THIS DIAGRAM MAKES IT CLEAR.

YES, I UNDERSTAND NOW.

ACCEPTED, PAULINE HAS STARTED ELEVEN WEEKS HARD TRAINING. SHE ATTENDS CLASSES TO LEARN ABOUT CATERING, HOW TO ATTEND TO SICK PASSENGERS, FASTEN SAFELY BELTS, MAKE PEOPLE COMFORTABLE AND BE CALM AND FRIENDLY UNDER ANY CIRCUMSTANCES.

HERE IS YOUR LUNCH, MADAM.

PART OF PAULINE'S TRAINING IS IN AN AIRCRAFT ON THE GROUND WHERE OTHER TRAINEES ACT AS PASSENGERS. HERE SHE LEARNS HOW TO BALANCE TRAYS OF FOOD AND DRINKS AND SERVE THE PASSENGERS WITHOUT STUMBLING.

GOOD-BYE, MARY. I HOPE YOU'LL COME ON MY PLANE AGAIN ONE DAY.

THANK YOU FOR LOOKING AFTER ME.

PAULINE HAS NOW COMPLETED HER FIRST FLIGHT AND IS SAYING FAREWELL TO HER PASSENGERS. HER JOB IS EXACTING AS WELL AS EXCITING, AND VERY DIFFICULT TO OBTAIN. IF *YOU* FEEL YOU WOULD QUALIFY FOR THIS SPECIALISED WORK, WE HOPE YOU'LL BE EVERY BIT AS HAPPY AS PAULINE.

I want to be a FLORIST

SUSAN IS VERY GOOD AT ARRANGING FLOWERS AND HAS BEEN TAKEN ON AS APPRENTICE TO A FLORIST. HER SALARY IS SMALL AND WILL REMAIN SO WHILE SHE IS BEING TRAINED.

AREN'T THESE ROSES LOVELY?

YES, SUSAN—AND YOU THREE ARE LEARNING VERY QUICKLY HOW TO WIRE THEM.

IT'S AMAZING HOW SOON ONE GETS USED TO IT.

WITH TWO OTHER GIRLS SUSAN IS BEING TAUGHT TO WIRE FLOWERS ARTISTICALLY FOR CORSAGES AND HEAD-DRESSES. THE TRADE NAME FOR THIS IS 'JEWELLERY'. LATER ON SHE WILL LEARN HOW TO MAKE UP BOUQUETS AND WREATHS.

NOW, SUSAN, YOUR JOB IS TO WRITE DOWN MY REMARKS AS FAST AS YOU CAN.

YES, MISS ASHTON. ISN'T THIS A BEAUTIFUL CHURCH?

SUSAN HAS BEEN CHOSEN FOR THE EXCITING JOB OF TAKING NOTES AND HELPING THE ASSISTANT FLORIST PLAN THE FLORAL DECORATIONS FOR A BIG SOCIETY WEDDING.

I WAS BEGINNING TO THINK YOU WEREN'T COMING IN THIS MORNING, SIR!

I'M LATE, AREN'T I? MY CAR BROKE DOWN.

HAVING BEEN WITH THE FIRM FOR THREE YEARS, SUSAN IS NOW IN THE SHOP LEARNING HOW TO SELL FLOWERS. SHE EARNS FOUR POUNDS A WEEK.

I'LL TAKE SIX DOZEN OF THOSE.

RIGHT, MISS!

SUSAN IS NOW ENTRUSTED WITH THE EXACTING TASK OF SELECTING AND BUYING FLOWERS FROM THE GROWERS. SHE HAS TO BE UP EARLY TO GET TO THE MARKET IN TIME AND MUST KNOW ALL ABOUT CURRENT PRICES.

I SEE YOUR OLD FIRM ARE DOING THE FLOWERS FOR THE EMBASSY BALL TOMORROW, SUSAN.

YES, I KNOW. I EXPECT THEY'LL LET ME HELP.

AFTER FIVE YEARS SUSAN HAS LEFT HER JOB AND DOES THE FLOWER ARRANGEMENTS AT A LARGE HOTEL. SUCH JOBS ARE FEW AND FAR BETWEEN, BUT SHE HAS WORKED HARD TO ACHIEVE HER AMBITION.

I want to be a SALESWOMAN

JENNIFER MASON LOVED TO PLAY 'SHOPS' WHEN SHE WAS A CHILD AND NOW THAT SHE'S LEFT SCHOOL SHE IS A JUNIOR SALESWOMAN IN A LOCAL STORE

I'M CHANGING OVER TO PERFUMERY TODAY. I WONDER HOW I SHALL GET ON WITH MISS THOMPSON?

YOU'LL BE ALL RIGHT, JENNIFER. HER BARK'S WORSE THAN HER BITE!

SMILE AT THE CUSTOMERS AND YOU'LL KEEP IN HER GOOD BOOKS.

JENNIFER HAS NOW BEEN AT THE STORE FOR SIX MONTHS. SHE TAKES TURNS IN SERVING IN THE VARIOUS DEPARTMENTS AND RECEIVES ABOUT THIRTY-FIVE SHILLINGS A WEEK BECAUSE SHE IS BEING TRAINED.

I'LL ATTEND TO HER WHILE YOU FINISH CHECKING THESE INVOICES.

MADAM WANTS TO KNOW IF WE SELL A STOCKING THAT'S FINER THAN THIS.

IN EACH DEPARTMENT JENNIFER WORKS UNDER THE SUPERVISION OF THE BUYER, WHOSE JOB IT IS TO TRAIN HER. JENNIFER LEARNS TO SERVE CUSTOMERS, TO SORT AND PUT AWAY NEW STOCK AND LIST INVOICES.

IN LONDON AND MOST OF THE PROVINCES EVENING CLASSES IN SALESMANSHIP ARE HELD IN THE TECHNICAL COLLEGES. JENNIFER IS NOW IN HER THIRD TERM AT ONE AND WILL TAKE AN EXAMINATION AT THE END OF IT.

AND IF YOU HAVEN'T THAT PARTICULAR ITEM IN STOCK OFFER YOUR CUSTOMER THE NEXT BEST THING—AND PERSUADE THEM TO BUY IT.

JENNIFER, HAS BEEN IN THE CHILDREN'S DEPARTMENT FOR TWO YEARS. SHE IS NOW FIRST SALESWOMAN AND EARNS FIVE POUNDS PER WEEK.

YOU ARE GOING TO BE A SMART GIRL! LET ME DO UP THIS BUTTON AND THEN YOU CAN SHOW MUMMY.

THAT SHADE OF RED SUITS HER VERY WELL. HAVE YOU A HAT IN THE SAME COLOUR?

IT'S TIME FOR YOU TO GO TO LUNCH NOW, MISS HARRIS.

SIGN PLEASE, MISS MASON.

JENNIFER HAS PASSED AN EXAM IN SALES MANAGEMENT AND IS NOW IN CHARGE OF A WHOLE DEPARTMENT. HER JOB IS A RESPONSIBLE ONE BECAUSE SHE HAS TO TRAIN OTHER GIRLS, BUT SHE IS WELL PAID AND VERY HAPPY.

I want to be a Dress Designer

Jill has always had a 'flair' for clothes. She has now enrolled for a three-year course in dress designing at her nearest Technical College.

AREN'T THE COLOURS SIMPLY WONDERFUL?

AND LOOK AT THE FOLDS IN THAT VELVET GOWN!

STUDENTS MUST HAVE A GOOD KNOWLEDGE OF PAST AND PRESENT DRESS STYLES, SO JILL GOES WITH HER FRIENDS TO ART GALLERIES AND MUSEUMS TO STUDY THE COLOUR AND DESIGN OF EVERY CENTURY.

THIS SILK MATERIAL IS AWFULLY DIFFICULT TO CUT.

I CAN ONLY LET YOU HAVE ANOTHER TEN MINUTES TO DO IT, JILL, SO FINISH AS QUICKLY AS YOU CAN.

JILL IS AT THE END OF HER SECOND YEAR. SHE IS CUTTING OUT A DRESS FROM A PATTERN THAT SHE HERSELF HAS DESIGNED, FOR SHE NEEDS TO KNOW ALL ABOUT THE PRACTICAL SIDE OF FASHIONS AS WELL.

... AND THIS EVENING GOWN CONCLUDES OUR SHOW FOR THIS AFTERNOON.

THE BIG DRESS HOUSES OFTEN INVITE TECHNICAL COLLEGE STUDENTS TO THEIR SHOWS. JILL LOVES TO GO, FOR SEEING THE MODEL DRESSES HELPS HER WITH HER OWN DESIGNING.

JILL IS VERY GOOD AT SKETCHING CLOTHES—AND DESIGNERS WITH THIS ABILITY CAN RISE VERY HIGH IN THEIR PROFESSION. SHE HAS NOW ALMOST FINISHED HER COURSE AND IS APPLYING FOR HER FIRST JOB.

CONGRATULATIONS, JILL—YOU'VE DESIGNED US A WINNER THIS TIME.

SHE CERTAINLY HAS!

THERE ARE VACANCIES FOR GOOD DESIGNERS IN THE WHOLESALE DRESS HOUSES WHICH SPECIALISE IN MASS PRODUCED CLOTHES. JILL HAS BEEN APPOINTED ASSISTANT DESIGNER FOR ONE AND RECEIVES A SALARY OF £300 WHICH WILL BE INCREASED EVERY YEAR.

I want to be a Personnel Officer

Felicity wants to be a personnel officer at a factory. The job requires a great deal of technical training and she is taking a two year course in Social Science at a University.

WHAT ABOUT A GAME OF TENNIS AFTER THIS LECTURE, FELICITY?

I'D LOVE IT!

I'LL GET HOLD OF JOHN AND SEE IF HE'LL MAKE UP A FOUR.

FELICITY IS IN HER SECOND YEAR AT UNIVERSITY. HER SYLLABUS INCLUDES INDUSTRIAL HISTORY AND LAW, SOCIAL ETHICS AND ADMINISTRATION, AND GENERAL AND INDUSTRIAL PSYCHOLOGY.

I'LL SEE THE SUPERVISOR AND ASK HER TO PUT YOU ON THE EARLY SHIFT, MRS HAINES.

THANK YOU, MISS. THEN I'LL BE ABLE TO LEAVE HOME WITH MY HUSBAND IN THE MORNINGS.

FEW PERSONNEL OFFICERS ARE UNDER TWENTY-ONE BECAUSE OF THE VARIED AND DIFFICULT PROBLEMS WITH WHICH THEY HAVE TO DEAL. FELICITY IS COPING WITH A PERSONAL ONE AT THE FACTORY WHERE SHE HAS JUST STARTED HER FIRST JOB.

THE ACCIDENT FIGURES ARE VERY LOW INDEED.

YES, THAT'S DUE TO THOSE NEW GUARDS WE HAD FITTED TO THE MACHINES.

SHE IS MAKING HER REGULAR TOUR OF THE PLANT WITH THE ASSISTANT MANAGER. IT IS PART OF A PERSONNEL OFFICER'S JOB TO SEE THAT THE RELATIONS BETWEEN THE WORKERS AND THE MANAGEMENT ARE FRIENDLY, FOR THIS IS ESSENTIAL TO THE SMOOTH RUNNING OF THE FACTORY.

THAT'S NINETEEN-FIFTEEN, HAVE YOU TIME TO FINISH THE GAME?

JUST ABOUT. THE BOARD MEETING'S NOT UNTIL TWO O'CLOCK.

FELICITY IS RESPONSIBLE FOR SEEING THAT THERE'S A RECREATION ROOM FOR THE FACTORY STAFF. THE CANTEEN, SICK CLUB, PERSONAL ADVICE SERVICE AND TRANSPORT ALSO COME UNDER HER CARE.

COMING OUT TO LUNCH, FELICITY?

YES— I'M ALMOST READY.

AFTER SEVEN YEARS FELICITY IS NOW SENIOR PERSONNEL OFFICER IN A LARGE INDUSTRIAL PLANT. SHE HAS A STAFF OF THREE TO HELP HER AND EARNS FIVE HUNDRED POUNDS A YEAR.

I want to be a COOK

SHEILA IS VERY GOOD AT MAKING PASTRY AND, WANTS TO LEARN HOW TO COOK REALLY WELL. SHE HAS BEEN ACCEPTED AT A COLLEGE NEAR HER HOME FOR AN EIGHTEEN MONTH DOMESTIC SCIENCE COURSE.

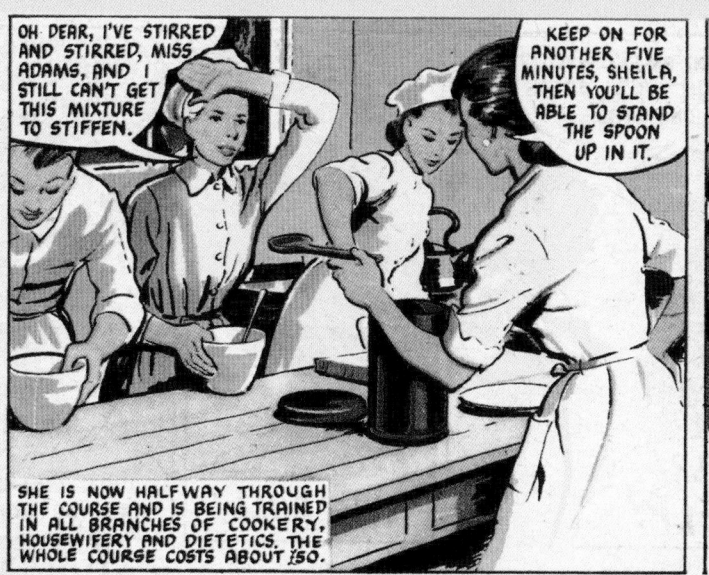

OH DEAR, I'VE STIRRED AND STIRRED, MISS ADAMS, AND I STILL CAN'T GET THIS MIXTURE TO STIFFEN.

KEEP ON FOR ANOTHER FIVE MINUTES, SHEILA, THEN YOU'LL BE ABLE TO STAND THE SPOON UP IN IT.

SHE IS NOW HALFWAY THROUGH THE COURSE AND IS BEING TRAINED IN ALL BRANCHES OF COOKERY, HOUSEWIFERY AND DIETETICS. THE WHOLE COURSE COSTS ABOUT £50.

BRIGHT EYES AND SHINING SCALES SHOW THAT THE FISH IS FRESH, GIRLS.

WHAT'S THE NAME OF THAT LARGE WHITE FISH OVER THERE, PLEASE?

ON TRIPS TO VARIOUS SHOPS SHEILA IS TAUGHT HOW TO CHOOSE FRESH FOOD, TO TELL THE DIFFERENCE BETWEEN TYPES OF GAME AND POULTRY AND ORDER FOR DINNER PARTIES OF EITHER FOUR, OR FOUR HUNDRED PEOPLE.

A LITTLE HEAT, A LOT OF PRACTICE AND — VOILA, SAUCE PIQUANTE!

SHEILA IS VERY INTERESTED IN LARGE SCALE CATERING AND NOW HER DOMESTIC SCIENCE COURSE IS OVER SHE HAS OBTAINED A POST AS JUNIOR CHEF AT A LARGE LONDON HOTEL.

THANK YOU, M'SIEU HENRI. THAT MAKES TWENTY THREE DIFFERENT SAUCES YOU'VE TAUGHT ME!

I SHALL BE PLEASED TO DEMONSTRATE THIS NEW MIXER TO ANY LADY IN HER OWN HOME.

ANXIOUS TO GET ON IN HER NEW JOB, SHEILA VISITS BIG STORES AND WATCHES DEMONSTRATIONS OF ALL NEW KITCHEN APPLIANCES. SHE IS STILL EMPLOYED AT THE HOTEL AND EARNS ABOUT THREE POUNDS A WEEK.

... AND NOW I WANT YOU TO GIVE THREE CHEERS FOR THE LADY WHO PREPARED THIS WONDERFUL PARTY.

SHEILA HAS NOW BEEN COOK AT A SMALL HOTEL FOR TWO YEARS. SHE IS VERY HAPPY AND HAS TWO OTHER GIRLS TO HELP HER IN THE KITCHEN. HER SALARY'S ABOUT FOUR POUNDS A WEEK PLUS ALL HER LIVING EXPENSES.

I want to be a TEACHER

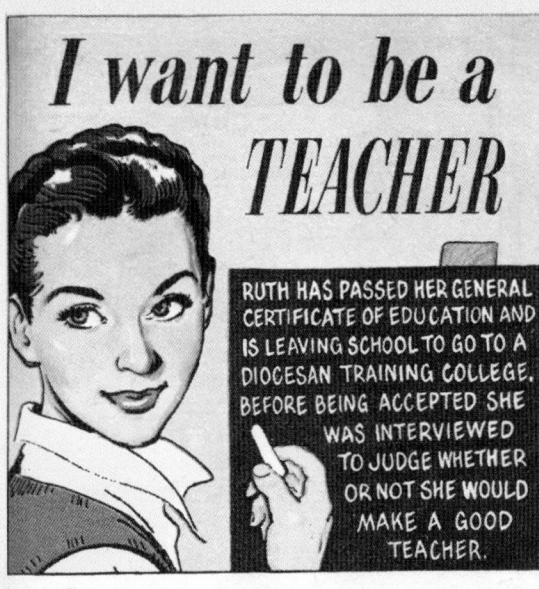

RUTH HAS PASSED HER GENERAL CERTIFICATE OF EDUCATION AND IS LEAVING SCHOOL TO GO TO A DIOCESAN TRAINING COLLEGE. BEFORE BEING ACCEPTED SHE WAS INTERVIEWED TO JUDGE WHETHER OR NOT SHE WOULD MAKE A GOOD TEACHER.

RUTH IS IN THE SECOND YEAR OF HER TWO YEARS' TRAINING AND STUDIES PRIMARY SCHOOL SUBJECTS AND PHYSICAL TRAINING. THIS TUITION IS FREE, BUT SHE PAYS FOR HER FOOD AND LODGING.

SHOOT, RUTH!

IF YOU GET THIS GOAL YOU'LL HAVE WON THE MATCH!

AS PART OF HER TRAINING RUTH GOES TO NEARBY PRIMARY SCHOOLS TO LEARN HOW TO HANDLE CLASSES BUT HER AMBITION IS TO TEACH INFANTS.

I WANT YOU TO SHOW MISS JONES WHAT A GOOD CLASS YOU CAN BE.

THIS IS MISS JONES, WHO HAS COME TO US THIS TERM TO TAKE OVER CLASS 1. I KNOW YOU WOULD LIKE ME TO WELCOME HER ON YOUR BEHALF.

THANK YOU VERY MUCH, MISS ADAMS.

HAVING FINISHED HER TRAINING RUTH TAKES OVER HER FIRST CLASS OF INFANTS. HER SALARY, FIXED BY THE BURNHAM COMMITTEE, STARTS AT £338 AND RISES ANNUALLY BY FIFTEEN POUNDS UP TO £504.

COME ON, ALL OF YOU—SING UP. YOUR MOTHERS WILL NEVER HEAR YOU IF YOU DON'T!

A PARENTS' OPEN DAY IS HELD IN THE SUMMER TERM AND RUTH IS REHEARSING HER CLASS FOR THEIR CONCERT. SHE IS LUCKY ENOUGH TO WORK IN A MODERN BUILDING WITH UP-TO-DATE EQUIPMENT. UNFORTUNATELY MANY SCHOOLS ARE STILL VERY OVERCROWDED.

RUTH, WHO LOVES HER JOB, SPENDS MOST EVENINGS PREPARING THE NEXT DAY'S WORK. SHE IS A MEMBER OF THE PARENT-TEACHER ASSN, AND TAKES AN ACTIVE PART IN THE SCHOOL DRAMATIC CLUB.

GOOD-BYE. GO HOME CAREFULLY.

IF YOU'RE READY TO LEAVE, RUTH, I'LL GIVE YOU A LIFT HOME.

I want to be a MILLINER

Brenda, who is very keen on fashion and is clever with her hands, wants to be a milliner. She is taking a course at a local Technical College.

I'VE BLOCKED IT THREE TIMES AND I STILL GET A BUMP ON THE CROWN!

THAT'S BECAUSE YOU TAKE IT OFF THE BLOCK TOO QUICKLY, BRENDA.

SHE LEARNS HOW TO BLOCK AND TRIM A VARIETY OF HATS. THE COURSE LASTS FOR TWO YEARS AND BRENDA IS GIVEN A GENERAL ART TRAINING BY QUALIFIED TEACHERS.

HAVING LEFT COLLEGE, BRENDA HAS BEGUN WORK IN A MILLINER'S SHOP NEAR HER HOME. AS AN APPRENTICE SHE EARNS THIRTY SHILLINGS A WEEK AND LEARNS ALL ABOUT THE SELLING SIDE OF THE HAT TRADE.

HMM, THIS IS RATHER TOO SEVERE FOR ME.

PERHAPS MADAM WOULD LIKE TO TRY THIS ONE?

BRENDA HAS NOW BEEN FOUR YEARS WITH THE FIRM AND EARNS £7 A WEEK. SHE IS ENCOURAGED TO SUBMIT HER OWN DESIGNS AND IS PAID A COMMISSION ON ANY SALES SHE MAKES.

I SKETCHED THREE HATS OVER THE WEEKEND, MISS LEYDON, AND THIS SEEMED TO ME TO BE THE BEST ONE.

YES, I LIKE IT. I'LL SEE WHAT MONSIEUR HENRI HAS TO SAY, BRENDA.

NOW A BUYER FOR HER FIRM, BRENDA ATTENDS HAT SHOWS REGULARLY. SHE EARNS TEN POUNDS A WEEK PLUS TRAVELLING EXPENSES, AND MAY HAVE THE CHANCE OF GOING ABROAD ON HER FIRM'S BEHALF LATER ON.

THAT SECOND ONE IS A SURE SELLER, DON'T YOU THINK?

YES. I'LL FIND OUT HOW MUCH THEY ARE ASKING FOR IT.

BRENDA HAS SAVED ENOUGH TO OPEN HER OWN MILLINERY SHOP WHERE SHE CAN DISPLAY HER ORIGINAL DESIGNS. THANKS TO HER GOOD TRAINING BRENDA'S CUSTOMERS COME BACK AGAIN AND AGAIN.

Brenda's

16

I MUST ADMIT YOU ALWAYS SEEM TO KNOW WHAT SUITS ME BEST.

GOOD-BYE, MRS OWEN. I'M SURE YOU'LL BE PLEASED WITH THE HAT.

I want to be a DOCTOR

BARBARA HAS DONE WELL AT SCHOOL AND NOW, THANKS TO HER PARENTS' GENEROSITY, IS LOOKING FORWARD TO HER FIVE YEARS' TRAINING IN MEDICINE

GOOD-BYE, BARBARA. WE WISH YOU EVERY SUCCESS.

THANK YOU VERY MUCH, MISS GREY. I'LL LET YOU KNOW HOW I GET ON.

FULL OF EXCITEMENT, BARBARA IS LEAVING SCHOOL TO ENTER A UNIVERSITY. SHE IS TO RECEIVE A COUNCIL GRANT TO HELP PAY FOR HER MEDICAL SCHOOL FEES, WHICH ARE VERY HIGH.

THE STUDY OF MEDICINE IS DIVIDED INTO THREE COURSES. BARBARA IS AT PRESENT IN THE MIDDLE OF HER PRE-MEDICAL COURSE WHICH WILL TAKE THREE TERMS. IT DEALS WITH THE STUDY OF BIOLOGY, CHEMISTRY AND PHYSICS.

... AND FROM THERE THE BLOOD PASSES TO THE LEFT VENTRICLE. IS THAT QUITE CLEAR?

YES, SIR.

ONE MORE SET, DAVID, AND THEN I REALLY MUST GO IN.

ALL RIGHT— ONE MORE IT IS, YOU STUDIOUS CREATURE!

BARBARA TAKES A PRECIOUS HOUR OFF FROM HER TEXT BOOKS TO PLAY TENNIS IN THE COLLEGE GROUNDS. PLACES AVAILABLE FOR WOMEN STUDENTS ARE STRICTLY LIMITED AND SHE IS DETERMINED TO QUALIFY AS SOON AS SHE CAN.

TELL ME, MISS DREW, WHAT SYMPTOMS ARE APPARENT TO YOU REGARDING THIS PATIENT?

HIS COLOUR IS POOR, SIR JAMES, AND HIS BREATHING IS LABOURED.

BARBARA HAS ALMOST COMPLETED HER CLINICAL COURSE, WHICH TAKES THREE YEARS. SHE IS 'WALKING THE WARDS' OF A FAMOUS HOSPITAL AND LEARNING ABOUT THE VARIOUS DISEASES AT FIRST HAND.

WELL, JENNIFER, YOU CAN GO HOME TOMORROW. WE'RE VERY PLEASED WITH YOU, AREN'T WE, SISTER?

YES, DR DREW. SHE HAS BEEN AN EXCELLENT PATIENT.

AFTER YEARS OF CONCENTRATED STUDY, BARBARA HAS QUALIFIED AS A MEDICAL PRACTITIONER. HER TRAINING HAS COST £200 A YEAR FOR FIVE YEARS AND SHE IS NOW IN HER FIRST JOB AS ASSISTANT TO THE HOSPITAL'S HONORARY PHYSICIAN.

I want to be a SPORTS MISTRESS

JOAN IS THE CHAMPION HOCKEY PLAYER OF HER YEAR AND THIS, PLUS A LOVE OF SWIMMING AND ATHLETICS, HAS MADE HER KEEN TO BE A SPORTS MISTRESS.

GOOD-BYE. I'LL PHONE YOU TONIGHT.

GOOD-BYE, JOAN. SAFE JOURNEY!

JOAN HAS OBTAINED HER GENERAL CERTIFICATE AND IS JUST OFF TO START A THREE YEAR COURSE AT A PHYSICAL TRAINING COLLEGE. THERE ARE EIGHT OF THESE COLLEGES IN GREAT BRITAIN AND THE FEES ARE £250 A YEAR.

A COURSE OF ANATOMY AND PHYSIOLOGY IS PART OF JOAN'S TRAINING AT THE COLLEGE. SHE WILL ALSO STUDY THE THEORY OF HEALTH EDUCATION AND EDUCATIONAL GYMNASTICS.

... AND THE INJURY TO THE ULNA NERVE RESULTS IN A PARTIAL PARALYSIS OF THE HAND.

YOUR SPEED IS EXCELLENT, JOAN, BUT YOUR STYLE NEEDS BRUSHING UP A BIT.

RIGHT-HO, I'LL TAKE IT A BIT SLOWER NEXT TIME.

JOAN IS NOW HALFWAY THROUGH HER THIRD YEAR AND IS CONCENTRATING ON GAMES, SWIMMING AND ATHLETICS, SINCE THESE ARE THE SUBJECTS SHE WANTS TO TEACH.

NOW A FULLY QUALIFIED PHYSICAL TRAINING TEACHER, JOAN IS APPLYING FOR THE POST OF SPORTS MISTRESS AT A LOCAL SECONDARY SCHOOL. IF ACCEPTED, SHE WILL BEGIN AT A SALARY OF £282 A YEAR, NON-RESIDENT.

GOSH, MOTHER, I'M NERVOUS! SUPPOSING THEY DON'T LIKE ME?

I'LL WAIT IN THE HALL FOR YOU. GOOD LUCK, DARLING.

JOAN HAS BEEN THE SCHOOL'S SPORTS MISTRESS FOR FIVE YEARS. HER SALARY IS NOW £400 A YEAR AND THIS, TOGETHER WITH THE LONG SCHOOL HOLIDAYS, ADDS TO THE ENJOYMENT OF HER JOB.

WELL PASSED. NOW GO ON, VALERIE—SHOOT!

I want to be a Market Gardener

DOROTHY LIVES IN THE COUNTRY AND HAS ALWAYS ENJOYED GARDENING. SHE IS GOING TO WORK IN A LARGE NURSERY NEAR HER HOME WHEN SHE LEAVES SCHOOL THIS TERM.

THREE MORE LECTURES, THEN THE EXAM. WHAT A GLOOMY PROSPECT.

CHEER UP! YOU OUGHT TO DO VERY WELL—YOU'RE KEEN ENOUGH.

DOROTHY ATTENDS LECTURES AT A LOCAL INSTITUTE AND, AFTER A TWO YEAR COURSE, IS TAKING AN EXAMINATION IN HORTICULTURE. THIS EXAM, WITH HER PRACTICAL EXPERIENCE, IS A VERY DESIRABLE QUALIFICATION.

THIS MUST BE THE BEST CROP OF STRAWBERRIES WE'VE HAD FOR A LONG TIME.

YES, IT'S CERTAINLY BEEN A WONDERFUL SUMMER SO FAR.

SHE HAS NOW PASSED HER EXAMINATION AND HAS BEEN WORKING IN THE NURSERY FOR THREE YEARS. HER WAGE IS THREE POUNDS A WEEK AND SHE IS LEARNING HOW TO MARKET THE PRODUCE.

THIS IS A FASCINATING OCCUPATION—THOUGH I NEVER THOUGHT I'D GET USED TO IT.

IT'S JUST A CASE OF THE BEES GETTING USED TO YOU, REALLY.

IN HER STUDIES DOROTHY INCLUDES A COURSE IN BEE-KEEPING AND FINDS IT AN ENTHRALLING OCCUPATION. SHE IS EARNING FOUR-POUNDS-TEN A WEEK AND IS ALREADY AN EXPERIENCED GARDENER.

... AND I HAVE PLEASURE IN PRESENTING THE CUP TO YOU FOR THE SECOND YEAR IN SUCCESSION!

THANK YOU VERY MUCH.

ON BEHALF OF HER FIRM, DOROTHY RECEIVES THE PRIZE FOR THE CHAMPION CHRYSANTHEMUM OF THE FLOWER SHOW. SHE FEELS JUSTLY PROUD OF THE PART SHE HAS PLAYED TOWARDS ITS CULTIVATION.

DOROTHY IS NOW RESPONSIBLE FOR THE GROUNDS OF A LARGE SCHOOL AND EARNS £450 PER ANNUM. HER WORK IS SATISFYING AND SHE HOPES, LATER, TO RUN HER OWN MARKET GARDEN.

WHAT ABOUT THOSE RUNNER BEANS? ARE THEY READY FOR PICKING?

YES, I CAN LET YOU HAVE THEM IN TIME FOR LUNCH TODAY.

I want to be a HAIRDRESSER

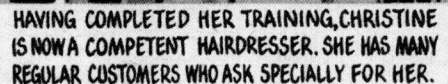

I want to be a Physiotherapist

A physiotherapist is someone who gives massage and electrical treatment. As Pamela has always been interested in helping sick people, this is what she is going to learn to do when she leaves school this term.

JUST TELL THE CLASS THAT FORMULA AGAIN, WILL YOU, PAMELA?

YES, MISS PALLETT.

PAMELA IS TAKING HER GENERAL CERTIFICATE OF EDUCATION AT SCHOOL THIS TERM. SHE WILL NEED TO PASS IN GENERAL SCIENCE, SO SHE IS STUDYING THIS SUBJECT EXTRA HARD.

I DO HOPE I CAN GO ON THE CHILDREN'S WARD TODAY.

I EXPECT MISS PRENTICE WILL LET YOU IF YOU ASK HER, PAMELA.

HAVING PASSED, PAMELA HAS NOW BEEN IN THE PHYSIOTHERAPY DEPARTMENT OF A LARGE HOSPITAL FOR THREE MONTHS. SHE IS TRAINED IN MASSAGE AND ELECTRICAL TREATMENT AND SPENDS SOME TIME ON THE HOSPITAL WARDS.

THRILLING TO THINK SHE'LL BE ABLE TO DANCE AGAIN, ISN'T IT?

SHE CERTAINLY HAD A VERY BAD ACCIDENT.

ONE OF US WILL PROBABLY BE GIVING HER TREATMENT TOMORROW.

PART OF PAMELA'S TRAINING CONSISTS OF WATCHING OPERATIONS AND ATTENDING DISSECTIONS AND ANATOMY CLASSES. DURING HER THREE YEARS' TRAINING SHE WILL SIT SEVERAL EXAMINATIONS, BOTH WRITTEN AND ORAL.

COME ON, STELLA. TRY AND STRAIGHTEN YOUR LEG JUST A LITTLE BIT MORE.

I'LL SOON BE ABLE TO TOUCH MY TOES, WON'T I?

PAMELA PARTICULARLY LIKES HER WORK AMONG CHILDREN. SHE IS NOW IN HER THIRD YEAR AND HAS HAD A FULL TRAINING IN ALL FORMS OF MASSAGE, ELECTRICAL AND RADIATION TREATMENTS.

NOW A CHARTERED PHYSIOTHERAPIST, PAMELA HAS GONE INTO PARTNERSHIP WITH AN OLDER WOMAN AND THEY HAVE BUILT UP A FLOURISHING PRACTICE.

I THINK ANOTHER TWO TREATMENTS WILL BE ENOUGH, MR LINDSAY.

THAT'S GOOD. I SHALL BE GLAD TO GET BACK TO WORK AGAIN.

I want to be a Fashion Artist

DENISE HAS A FLAIR FOR SKETCHING CLOTHES AND HOPES TO BECOME A FASHION ARTIST. SHE IS GOING TO A SCHOOL OF ART FOR THREE YEARS TRAINING.

THAT'S COMING ON NICELY, DENISE. YOU'RE STILL RATHER HEAVY ON THE OUTLINE, THOUGH.

THANK YOU, MISS REYNOLDS.

NOW IN HER SECOND YEAR, DENISE IS VERY HAPPY AT THE SCHOOL. THE FEES ARE NOT HIGH, BUT SHE HAS TO PROVIDE HER OWN MATERIALS FOR DRAWING AND PAINTING.

DENISE HAS FINISHED HER COURSE AND IS HAVING A HOLIDAY BEFORE BEGINNING HER NEW JOB WITH A DRESS HOUSE. AS A JUNIOR THERE SHE WILL EARN ONLY A GUINEA A WEEK FOR THE FIRST THREE MONTHS.

THERE, MOTHER, I'VE DESIGNED YOU A REALLY STUNNING SUIT.

"STUNNING" IS THE WORD! IT'S MUCH TOO SMART FOR COUNTRY WALKS.

IT IS A REALLY BEAUTIFUL MATERIAL, MADAME.

I WONDER IF IT WILL LOOK AS GOOD AS THE SKETCH DOES WHEN IT IS MADE UP?

PART OF DENISE'S JOB IS TO MAKE A QUICK SKETCH OF A GOWN FOR A CUSTOMER, SO THAT SHE WILL HAVE SOME IDEA OF HOW THE FINISHED GARMENT WILL LOOK.

DENISE IS OFTEN SENT TO TRADE SHOWS TO SKETCH DRESSES FOR THE DAILY PAPERS. SHE ALSO HAS MANY OPPORTUNITIES FOR VISITING FAMOUS DRESS HOUSES ABROAD.

THIS DRESS HAS THE VERY LATEST DRAPED LINE . . .

I WANT YOU TO LOOK AT SOME NEW FASHION PHOTOGRAPHS TOMORROW, DENISE.

SORRY, SIMON, I'M OFF TO PARIS IN THE MORNING.

HER BRILLIANT SKETCHES AND ENTHUSIASM HAVE LANDED DENISE AT THE TOP OF A VERY EXACTING PROFESSION. SHE IS NOW THE FASHION EDITOR OF A WOMAN'S MAGAZINE.

I want to be a POLICE-WOMAN

JILL'S FATHER IS AN INSPECTOR OF POLICE AND SHE IS KEEN TO 'FOLLOW IN HIS FOOTSTEPS' BY BECOMING A POLICEWOMAN.

THE MINIMUM AGE FOR ENTRY IS TWENTY-TWO, SO JILL IS FILLING IN TIME BY WORKING AS A CLERK IN SCOTLAND YARD. ALL SHE LEARNS THERE WILL STAND HER IN GOOD STEAD LATER ON.

HAVING REACHED THE QUALIFYING AGE, JILL HAS BEEN ACCEPTED FOR THE METROPOLITIAN POLICE AND BEGINS A THREE MONTHS' TRAINING AT PEEL HOUSE, LONDON. SHE RECEIVES £355 A YEAR AND HER UNIFORM, WHICH IS MADE TO HER OWN MEASUREMENTS.

JILL IS NOW DOING PATROL DUTIES UNDER THE SUPERVISION OF AN EXPERIENCED POLICE-WOMAN. SHE WORKS A DAILY TOUR OF EIGHT HOURS, WITH ONE HOUR FOR REFRESHMENTS.

BECAUSE JILL OFTEN HAS TO APPEAR IN COURT, SHE HAS HAD A FULL TRAINING IN COURT PROCEDURE AND CAN GIVE HER EVIDENCE CLEARLY AND CONCISELY.

JILL HAS COMPLETED FOUR YEARS AS A POLICE-WOMAN AND IS TAKING A TECHNICAL EXAMINATION TO BECOME A SERGEANT. SHE HOPES TO JOIN THE CRIMINAL INVESTIGATION DEPARTMENT LATER ON, WHERE HER WORK MAY BE EVEN MORE INTERESTING.

I want to be an ACTRESS

CAROL HAS ALWAYS ENJOYED AMATEUR THEATRICALS AND WHEN SHE LEAVES SCHOOL SHE HOPES TO TRAIN TO BE AN ACTRESS.

SHE HAS BEEN EXTREMELY LUCKY AND OBTAINED A PLACE AT A FAMOUS SCHOOL OF DRAMATIC ART. HER COURSE THERE WILL LAST TWO YEARS AND COST ABOUT £150 NON-RESIDENT. GRANTS ARE AVAILABLE FOR OUTSTANDING STUDENTS.

THE INTENSIVE COURSE INCLUDES SPEECH TRAINING AND DEPORTMENT UNDER QUALIFIED INSTRUCTORS. CAROL HAS OBTAINED LODGINGS IN A STUDENTS' HOSTEL NEAR THE SCHOOL, WHERE SHE SHARES A BED-SITTING ROOM WITH A FRIEND.

CAROL GOES AS OFTEN AS SHE CAN TO WATCH THE PERFORMANCES OF GREAT ACTORS AND ACTRESSES. THIS IS ALL PART OF THE TRAINING, AND SHE AND OTHER STUDENTS LEARN MUCH THAT WILL HELP THEM WITH THEIR OWN CAREERS.

HAVING COMPLETED TWO YEARS AT THE SCHOOL, CAROL HAS NOW JOINED A REPERTORY COMPANY. THEY HAVE BEGUN THEIR WINTER SEASON OF PLAYS AND SHE IS GIVEN SMALL PARTS WITH ONE OR TWO LINES TO SAY.

CAROL HAS BEEN WORKING HARD ON TOUR FOR THREE YEARS AND HAS AT LAST BEEN GIVEN THE 'LEAD' IN A PLAY BY A FAMOUS WRITER. LIKE ALL OTHER ASPIRING ACTRESSES, SHE HOPES ONE DAY AN EMINENT PRODUCER WILL 'SPOT' HER AND MAKE HER FAMOUS.

I want to be an ALMONER

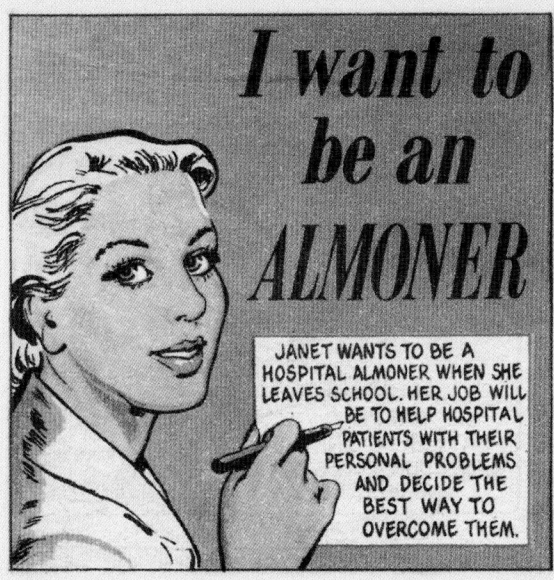

JANET WANTS TO BE A HOSPITAL ALMONER WHEN SHE LEAVES SCHOOL. HER JOB WILL BE TO HELP HOSPITAL PATIENTS WITH THEIR PERSONAL PROBLEMS AND DECIDE THE BEST WAY TO OVERCOME THEM.

SHE HAS PASSED HER G.C.E. EXAM (WITH TWO SUBJECTS AT 'A' LEVEL) SO THAT SHE WILL BE ABLE TO TAKE A SOCIAL SCIENCE DIPLOMA AT A UNIVERSITY WHEN SHE IS NINETEEN. UNTIL THEN, SHE IS WORKING FOR HER LOCAL DENTIST.

IS IT MY TURN NEXT, MISS?

YES, TOMMY, YOU CAN COME IN NOW.

STUDENTS TRAIN AT A HOSPITAL AND THE WHOLE COURSE LASTS A YEAR.

SO I WOULD BE A STUDENT ALMONER DURING THAT TIME?

JANET, NOW TWENTY-ONE, HAS GAINED HER DIPLOMA AND NEXT IS GOING TO TRAIN FOR THE CERTIFICATE OF THE INSTITUTE OF ALMONERS. THIS TRAINING COSTS ABOUT 85 GUINEAS, BUT LOCAL EDUCATION AUTHORITY GRANTS ARE AVAILABLE. SHE IS HERE BEING INTER-VIEWED BY THE SELECTION BOARD.

DURING HER TRAINING AT THE HOSPITAL JANET LEARNS THE PRACTICAL SIDE OF HER WORK BY VISITING THE PATIENTS THERE. SHE ALSO ATTENDS THE INSTITUTE FOR LECTURES AND DISCUSSIONS.

DON'T WORRY, MRS WOOD, JUST HURRY UP AND GET WELL AGAIN.

WE'LL COME TO SEE YOU AGAIN TOMORROW.

GOSH, IT'S GOOD TO BE HOME AGAIN, DADDY.

YOU WERE LUCKY TO GET THAT POST AT THE LOCAL HOSPITAL, JANET.

YES, YOU'LL BE ABLE TO LIVE WITH US TOO.

JANET'S TRAINING IS COMPLETED AND SHE HAS GAINED HER ALMONER'S CERTIFICATE. HER FIRST POST IS AT A HOSPITAL NEAR HER HOME, WHERE SHE WILL BE ASSISTANT ALMONER WITH A STARTING SALARY OF £410. THIS WILL BE INCREASED YEARLY.

JANET IS EXTREMELY HAPPY IN HER JOB, WHERE SHE MEETS ALL SORTS OF PEOPLE AND HELPS THEM WITH THEIR PROBLEMS. A HEAD ALMONER IN ONE OF THE BIG COLLEGE HOSPITALS CAN COMMAND A SALARY OF £700 A YEAR.

... AND YOU CAN SAFELY LEAVE THE BABY IN THE CRÈCHE WHILE YOU COME FOR TREATMENT.

EXCUSE ME. CAN YOU LET ME HAVE THAT CASE SHEET I ASKED FOR THIS MORNING, JANET?

I want to be a Chartered Accountant

MATHS ARE EDNA'S BEST SUBJECT AND WHEN SHE LEAVES SCHOOL THIS TERM SHE IS TO BEGIN HER TRAINING AS A CHARTERED ACCOUNTANT.

THAT'S ALL SETTLED THEN, MRS LEIGH?

IN A PROFESSION WHICH IS MAINLY OPEN TO MEN, EDNA HAS BEEN LUCKY ENOUGH TO BE TAKEN ON AS A PUPIL WITH A FIRM OF CHARTERED ACCOUNTANTS. SHE WILL TRAIN THERE FOR FIVE YEARS.

YES, MR CRAWFORD. MY DAUGHTER WILL START WORK WITH YOU ON MONDAY AT NINE O'CLOCK.

THANK GOODNESS THAT'S OVER! NOW FOR THE RESULTS.

I HOPE WE'VE PASSED, EDNA. I WONDER HOW LONG WE WILL HAVE TO WAIT BEFORE WE KNOW?

EDNA HAS ALREADY SAT AND PASSED HER PRELIMINARY EXAM FOR THE INSTITUTE OF CHARTERED ACCOUNTANTS. SHE HAS NOW TAKEN THE INTERMEDIATE EXAM AND WILL GO ON TO THE FINAL. THE COST OF THE THREE EXAMS IS TWELVE GUINEAS.

KNOWING THAT THE FINAL EXAMINATION IS THE MOST DIFFICULT, EDNA IS STUDYING HARD IN HER SPARE TIME. SHE IS ALSO BEING COACHED PRIVATELY, FOR SHE MUST HAVE A THOROUGH KNOWLEDGE OF COMMERCIAL AND COMPANY LAW AND TAXATION.

COME ALONG, DEAR—IT'S TEN O'CLOCK AND TIME TO STOP STUDYING.

RIGHT-HO, MOTHER. ONE MORE ENTRY AND THEN I'VE FINISHED.

THANK YOU FOR CLEARING UP THAT POINT ABOUT OUR INCOME TAX, MISS LEIGH.

I'M GLAD I'VE BEEN ABLE TO HELP YOU.

HAVING PASSED ALL HER EXAMS AND FINISHED HER FIVE YEARS' TRAINING, EDNA IS NOW A MEMBER OF THE INSTITUTE OF CHARTERED ACCOUNTANTS. SHE HAS BEEN GIVEN A POSITION OF RESPONSIBILITY WITH HER FIRM

JUMP IN, EDNA, AND I'LL DRIVE YOU HOME.

THAT WOULD BE WONDERFUL. I'M LATE TONIGHT BECAUSE WE'RE SNOWED UNDER WITH WORK.

EDNA IS VERY HAPPY AMONGST ALL THE FACTS AND FIGURES WHICH MAKE UP HER JOB AND, ALTHOUGH SHE HAS HAD TO WORK HARD FOR SUCCESS, MANY INTERESTING AND WELL-PAID JOBS WILL BE OPEN TO HER IN THE FUTURE.

I want to be a Continuity Girl

Linda is very observant and has a good memory. She can do high-speed shorthand and typing and hopes to become a continuity girl in a film studio.

AH, IS THAT THE SCRIPT OF THE DOCUMENTARY FILM I ASKED FOR?

YES, AND IT'S ALL COMPLETE.

SO THAT SHE CAN GET TO KNOW ALL ABOUT FILM-MAKING, LINDA HAS TAKEN A CLERK'S POST IN A STUDIO. HERE SHE LEARNS TO FILE THE VARIOUS FILM SCRIPTS CORRECTLY AND SOMETIMES FETCHES AND CARRIES FOR THE MEN ON THE SET.

THAT OTHER FAN WAS THE WRONG COLOUR. THEY WANT THIS BLUE ONE.

TAKE IT DOWN THEN, WILL YOU, LINDA?

AFTER THREE YEARS LINDA'S QUICK BRAIN HAS EARNED HER THE JOB OF ASSISTANT TO THE CONTINUITY GIRL. HERE SHE IS FETCHING AN ITEM FROM THE PROPERTY ROOM—FOR, WHEN THE SAME SCENE TAKES SOME TIME TO SHOOT, THE CHARACTERS MUST BE DRESSED IN EXACTLY THE SAME CLOTHES EACH DAY.

HOW LONG WAS THAT SHOT, LINDA?

TWO MINUTES AND THIRTY SECONDS, MR JACOBS.

ONE OF LINDA'S MANY JOBS IS TO ACCOUNT FOR EVERY MINUTE SPENT ON THE SET TO CHECK POSSIBLE WASTE OF TIME AND MONEY. SHE TIMES EVERY SCENE WITH A STOP-WATCH AND MAKES NOTES FOR THE FILM EDITOR.

HOPE EVERYTHING GOES WELL TODAY, LINDA.

MORNING MISS, MORNING SIR.

I DO TOO, MIKE! THANKS FOR THE LIFT.

AFTER FOUR MORE YEARS LINDA IS RATHER NERVOUSLY BEGINNING HER FIRST DAY AS A CONTINUITY GIRL. SHE ACTS AS A SORT OF SECRETARY TO THE FILM ITSELF AND IS ANSWERABLE FOR ANY MISTAKES IN THE SEQUENCE.

MR OLIVER CAME IN THROUGH THE OTHER DOOR YESTERDAY, MAC.

SO HE DID. GOOD GIRL, LINDA— WE'LL SHOOT THAT SCENE AGAIN.

NOW FULLY TRAINED, LINDA IS HAPPY AND CONFIDENT IN HER JOB. VACANCIES FOR THIS WORK SELDOM OCCUR, BUT IF YOU ARE LUCKY ENOUGH TO FIND ONE WE WISH YOU EVERY SUCCESS.

I want to be a CLUB LEADER

Mary Andrews always enjoyed visiting her youth club and now she has her General Certificate of Education she is going to University to take a two-year course in social studies

THIS IS THE BOOK I WAS TELLING YOU ABOUT, MARY. I KNOW YOU'LL LIKE IT.

THANKS, JOE. I'LL READ IT TONIGHT.

AT THE UNIVERSITY, MARY ATTENDS MANY LECTURES AND DISCUSSIONS. THE LIFE THERE IS FULL AND EXCITING AND, BECAUSE THEY ARE SO KEEN ON THEIR TRAINING, MARY AND THE OTHER STUDENTS STUDY IN THEIR SPARE TIME.

I SPOKE MY LINES TOO FAST THAT TIME, DIDN'T I?

YES, YOU MUST LEARN TO TAKE THEM MORE SLOWLY SO THAT EVERYONE IN THE AUDIENCE WILL BE ABLE TO HEAR.

HAVING FINISHED HER COURSE AT THE UNIVERSITY, MARY IS NOW DOING SIX MONTHS PRACTICAL TRAINING. THIS COVERS ALL FORMS OF CLUB MANAGEMENT AND INCLUDES A STUDY OF SUBJECTS — LIKE DRAMATICS — IN WHICH MANY OF THE YOUNG PEOPLE MARY WILL BE MIXING WITH WILL BE INTERESTED.

THEY SEEM TO BE HAVING A WONDERFUL TIME.

YES—AND THEY ORGANISED IT ALL THEMSELVES WITH MY HELP.

AS PART OF HER PRACTICAL TRAINING MARY WORKS WITH SHEILA, AN EXPERIENCED CLUB LEADER. THEY ARE SPENDING THE EVENING AT SHEILA'S CLUB AND FROM HER MARY LEARNS HOW TO ORGANISE ALL THE DIFFERENT CLUB ACTIVITIES.

AS IT'S SUCH A LOVELY DAY WE'LL CYCLE DOWN TO THE SEA. WOULD YOU LIKE THAT?

THAT WILL BE SUPER, MISS ANDREWS!

MARY IS NOW FULLY TRAINED AND HAS TAKEN OVER A CLUB OF HER OWN. SHE SPENDS FIVE EVENINGS THERE EACH WEEK— AND NOW SHE'S OFF WITH HER MEMBERS ON A SATURDAY AFTERNOON CYCLE RUN.

MAY I SPEAK TO YOU FOR A MOMENT, MISS ANDREWS?

CERTAINLY, JUNE—COME ON IN.

THANKS TO MARY'S INFLUENCE, MEMBERS COME TO HER FOR HELP AND ADVICE. MANY OF THEM ARE KEEN TO DO EXTRA CLUB WORK, SO SHE IS ABLE TO TELL THEM ALL ABOUT THE SPECIAL TRAINING COURSE FOR SENIOR MEMBERS.

I want to be an Architect

PEGGY DESIGNED HER OWN DOLL'S HOUSE AS A CHILD AND WHEN SHE LEAVES SCHOOL THIS TERM SHE IS GOING TO TRAIN TO BE AN ARCHITECT.

I'VE JUST HEARD THAT OUR FIRM HAS LANDED THE CONTRACT TO DESIGN A NEW BLOCK OF OFFICES.

GOODY! PERHAPS WE'LL BE ALLOWED TO HELP.

PEGGY HAS BEGUN HER CAREER AS A JUNIOR ASSISTANT IN HER LOCAL ARCHITECT'S OFFICE AND ATTENDS AN EVENING COURSE IN ARCHITECTURE AT THE POLYTECHNIC. THERE IS A FIVE YEAR FULL-TIME UNIVERSITY COURSE, BUT PEGGY CANNOT AFFORD THIS.

AFTER 3 YEARS PEGGY HAS BEEN GIVEN MORE IMPORTANT WORK TO DO AND SOMETIMES GOES ON A SURVEYING JOB WITH A QUALIFIED ARCHITECT. IN 4 YEARS' TIME SHE HOPES TO TAKE THE FINAL EXAM FOR HER A.R.I.B.A.

SORRY, PEGGY. ALTER THAT LAST MEASUREMENT BY A YARD, WILL YOU?

RIGHT— THAT MAKES IT A HUNDRED AND TWO YARDS.

THERE, DADDY— WHAT ABOUT A HOUSE LIKE THAT?

VERY NICE, PEGGY, BUT I'D NEED TO BE A MILLIONAIRE TO PAY FOR IT!

WHY NOT TRY DESIGNING ONE WE COULD AFFORD?

PEGGY HAS WORKED HARD AND PASSED HER FINAL EXAM. SHE HAS NOW OBTAINED THE POST OF ASSISTANT ARCHITECT IN A CITY ARCHITECT'S OFFICE AND EARNS ABOUT £350 A YEAR.

MISS REID, LET ME HAVE THE WORKING DRAWINGS OF THE CLARENCE STREET FLATS, WILL YOU?

YES, RIGHT AWAY, MR GIRLING.

AFTER THREE MORE YEARS PEGGY'S SALARY HAS BEEN INCREASED AND SHE HAS AN OFFICE OF HER OWN. SHE IS REQUIRED TO MAKE WORKING DRAWINGS AND WRITTEN SPECIFICATIONS FOR THE NEW BUILDINGS DESIGNED BY HER FIRM.

WELL, PEGGY, THOSE FLATS CERTAINLY LOOK GOOD, DON'T THEY?

YES, AND THEY'RE JUST AS NICE INSIDE, WHICH IS MORE IMPORTANT.

PEGGY HAS REALISED HER SCHOOLGIRL AMBITION, IS NOW A COMPETENT ARCHITECT AND HAS THE PLEASURE OF SEEING FLATS AND BUILDINGS THAT SHE HAS HELPED TO DESIGN COME TO LIFE.

I want to be a PHOTO-GRAPHER

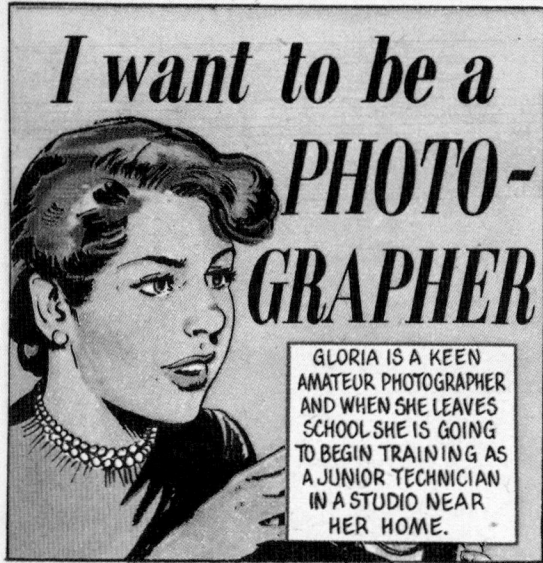

GLORIA IS A KEEN AMATEUR PHOTOGRAPHER AND WHEN SHE LEAVES SCHOOL SHE IS GOING TO BEGIN TRAINING AS A JUNIOR TECHNICIAN IN A STUDIO NEAR HER HOME.

THESE PROOFS OF THE COUNTY SPORTS CHAMPIONSHIPS HAVE COME UP WELL.

GOOD! THAT'LL PLEASE A FEW HUNDRED PEOPLE.

THERE ARE NOT MANY WOMEN EMPLOYED IN PHOTOGRAPHY. GLORIA IS LUCKY ENOUGH TO WORK IN A SMALL PRIVATE STUDIO WHERE SHE HAS A CHANCE TO LEARN ALL THE ASPECTS OF THE CRAFT. AT PRESENT SHE IS LEARNING HOW TO DEVELOP AND PRINT FILMS.

SHE IS NOW LEARNING HOW TO 'TOUCH UP' PHOTOGRAPHS AND PAINT THEM TO CUSTOMERS' REQUIREMENTS. SHE FINDS HER WORK ABSORBING AND IS KEEN TO GET ON. SHE EARNS THREE POUNDS PER WEEK AND IS IN HER SECOND YEAR.

IT'S CERTAINLY A TRICKY BUSINESS PAINTING IN EYELASHES.

YOU'RE GETTING ALONG WELL. YOU'VE GOT A VERY STEADY HAND.

GLORIA, WILL YOU COME TO THE COLLEGE DANCE WITH ME NEXT SATURDAY?

THANK YOU, PAUL, I SHOULD LIKE TO VERY MUCH.

GLORIA IS ATTENDING EVENING CLASSES IN PHOTOGRAPHY AT A TECHNICAL COLLEGE. SHE WILL TAKE A THREE-TERM COURSE AND LATER SIT FOR AN EXAMINATION SET BY THE INSTITUTE OF BRITISH PHOTOGRAPHERS.

THERE YOU ARE, ROGER. YOU HOLD THIS AND WATCH THE BIRDIE.

A LITTLE MORE LIGHT ON THE LEFT PLEASE, GLORIA.

SHE IS NOW AN ASSISTANT PHOTOGRAPHER IN THE STUDIO. SHE HAS TO KNOW HOW TO LIGHT AND GROUP HER CLIENTS. SHE RECEIVES SIX POUNDS PER WEEK AND HAS RECENTLY OBTAINED AN I.B.P. DIPLOMA, WHICH IS ESSENTIAL TO HER CAREER.

GLORIA, I'VE LEFT A COUPLE OF FILMS UPSTAIRS FOR YOU. HOW LONG BEFORE I CAN HAVE THE PRINTS?

I'LL START ON THEM RIGHT AWAY, ROGER, AND BRING THEM DOWN.

THAT'S FINE. THANKS A LOT.

AFTER TEN YEARS, GLORIA HAS LEFT THE STUDIO AND IS NOW WORKING AS A PHOTOGRAPHER IN A LARGE PRESS OFFICE. SHE RECEIVES £750 A YEAR AND ENJOYS THE BUSY, VARIED LIFE OF THE OFFICE.

I want to be an Interior Designer

VIRGINIA IS ALWAYS CHANGING ROUND THE FURNITURE IN HER BEDROOM AND PLANNING NEW COLOUR SCHEMES FOR IT. WHEN SHE LEAVES SCHOOL SHE WANTS TO TRAIN AS AN INTERIOR DESIGNER.

YOUR CLAY'S NOT QUITE WET ENOUGH, VIRGINIA.

OH, SO *THAT'S* WHY IT'S HARD TO GET SOME SHAPE INTO IT!

SHE IS TAKING A GENERAL TWO-YEAR ART COURSE AT HER LOCAL ART SCHOOL. THIS IS ESSENTIAL, AS VIRGINIA WANTS TO TAKE THE INTERMEDIATE EXAMINATION OF THE CITY AND GUILDS OF LONDON INSTITUTE.

THAT'S MY PROBLEM. NOW WHAT WOULD YOU HAVE DONE?

HAVING PASSED HER INTERMEDIATE EXAM, VIRGINIA IS TAKING A FURTHER THREE-YEAR COURSE AT ART SCHOOL IN INTERIOR DESIGN. CLASSES ARE GIVEN BY DESIGNERS, WHO SET THE STUDENTS PROBLEMS THEY HAVE MET THEMSELVES.

ON FREE AFTERNOONS, VIRGINIA GOES TO EXHIBITIONS OF CONTEMPORARY FURNITURE, WHICH SHE IS STUDYING AND LEARNING TO MAKE AT THE SCHOOL. OTHER SUBJECTS INCLUDE METAL WORK, WOOD WORK, PRACTICAL PAINTING AND USE OF COLOUR.

THIS PIECE OF FURNITURE IS NICELY FINISHED, RUTH.

YES, BUT I'D PREFER A SLIGHTLY DARKER WOOD.

GO ON INTO THE FOYER, VIRGINIA. I'LL BE WITH YOU IN A MOMENT.

GOSH, THIS IS THRILLING!

AS A REWARD FOR PASSING HER FINAL EXAM, VIRGINIA IS ENJOYING A NIGHT AT THE THEATRE WITH HER FATHER BEFORE SHE STARTS HER FIRST JOB.

THE ROOM IS LARGE, SO YOU'LL HAVE LOTS OF SCOPE.

VIRGINIA HAS BEEN LUCKY ENOUGH TO FIND A POSITION AS ASSISTANT IN AN ARCHITECT'S OFFICE AND IS OFTEN ASKED TO DESIGN SPECIAL FURNITURE WHICH WILL SUIT THE PROJECT UPON WHICH THE ARCHITECT HIMSELF IS WORKING.

I want to be a Pharmacist

ANNE'S BEST SUBJECT AT SCHOOL IS SCIENCE. SHE HAS PASSED HER GENERAL CERTIFICATE OF EDUCATION IN THE NECESSARY SUBJECTS AND WANTS TO BEGIN TRAINING AS A PHARMACIST.

WHAT ARE THE LECTURES THIS MORNING? I FORGOT TO LOOK AT THE NOTICE-BOARD.

PHYSIOLOGY'S FIRST, ANNE. THEN WE HAVE TWO HOURS OF CHEMISTRY.

ANNE HAS PASSED THE PHARMACEUTICAL SOCIETY'S INTERMEDIATE EXAMINATION. SHE IS NOW TAKING A TWO YEARS' COURSE OF STUDY AT A SCHOOL OF PHARMACY FOR THE QUALIFYING EXAMINATION.

AS WELL AS ATTENDING LECTURES, ANNE DOES PRACTICAL WORK IN THE LABORATORY. SHE IS STUDYING BACTERIOLOGY, PHYSIOLOGY AND ANALYTICAL CHEMISTRY IN THIS WAY, AND LEARNING ALL ABOUT DRUGS AND OTHER MEDICINAL SUBSTANCES.

THIS SLIDE'S A BIT TRICKY. WOULD YOU HELP ME FOCUS IT, PLEASE?

THIS IS THE MEDICINE FOR MRS BOOTH IN WARD 6.

THANK YOU, ANNE. IT'S MOST URGENT.

HAVING PASSED HER FINAL EXAMINATION, ANNE GOES ON TO TAKE A YEAR'S PRACTICAL TRAINING IN THE PHARMACEUTICAL DEPARTMENT OF A LARGE HOSPITAL BEFORE BEING REGISTERED AS A PHARMACIST.

OUR STOCKS OF TINCTURES ARE GETTING LOW.

YES, WE MUST ORDER MORE FROM THE MANUFACTURER.

IN ADDITION TO DISPENSING FOR THE PATIENTS IN THE HOSPITAL, ANNE LOOKS AFTER THE SUPPLIES OF DRUGS AND DRESSINGS, AND ORDERS MORE WHEN NECESSARY.

ANNE, CONFIDENT AND HAPPY AT HER JOB, IS NOW EMPLOYED IN A CHEMIST'S SHOP. SHE IS RESPONSIBLE FOR DISPENSING PRESCRIPTIONS BROUGHT INTO THE SHOP AND ALSO ATTENDS TO THE CUSTOMERS. HER SALARY IS £500 A YEAR AND THIS WILL BE INCREASED AS SHE BECOMES MORE EXPERIENCED.

GOOD MORNING, ANNE. YOU'VE A BUSY DAY AHEAD OF YOU, I THINK.

RIGHT, MR PERKINS. THEN I'LL GET TO WORK STRAIGHT AWAY.

I want to be a Journalist

KAY'S BEST SUBJECT IS ENGLISH. SHE IS LIVELY AND INTELLIGENT AND HOPES ONE DAY TO BECOME A NEWSPAPER REPORTER.

DOUBLE-SPACED TYPING LOOKS NEATER AND IS MORE LEGIBLE, KAY. TRY IT LIKE THAT.

A KNOWLEDGE OF SHORT-HAND AND TYPING IS ESSENTIAL TO A JOURNALIST, SO KAY IS TAKING A COURSE AT NIGHT SCHOOL. SHE FINISHES SCHOOL THIS TERM AND HAS APPLIED FOR A JOB IN THE OFFICE OF HER LOCAL NEWSPAPER.

YES, MISS ROWE, I WILL.

KAY READS AS MUCH CURRENT LITERATURE AS SHE CAN, FOR KNOWING EXACTLY WHAT TYPE OF STORIES AND ARTICLES THE NEWSPAPERS PRINT IS PART OF THE STOCK-IN-TRADE OF A JOURNALIST.

HERE YOU ARE, SIS. I SCROUNGED ALL THESE FOR YOU.

GOSH, WHAT A PILE! THANKS A LOT, JIMMY.

SHE HAS BEEN WITH THE NEWSPAPER FOR TWO YEARS NOW. SHE EARNS SIX POUNDS A WEEK AND HAS LEARNED HOW TO WRITE UP 'COPY'. HER HOURS ARE VERY INDEFINITE AND SHE OFTEN HAS TO WORK IN THE EVENINGS AND AT WEEK-ENDS.

...AND SHE WAS ATTENDED BY TWO BRIDESMAIDS AND A PAGE.

THAT'S THE FIFTH WEDDING REPORT THAT'S COME IN THIS MORNING.

I'VE GOT TO RETURN TO THE OFFICE NOW, KAY, BUT I'LL COME BACK AGAIN BEFORE LUNCH.

RIGHT-HO, PETER.

KAY INTENDS TO STAY ON THE REPORTING SIDE OF JOURNALISM, SO SHE COVERS AS MANY COURT CASES, WEDDINGS AND OTHER ACTIVITIES AS SHE CAN. SHE HAS NOW COMPLETED FIVE YEARS ON THE SAME LOCAL DAILY PAPER AND IS ANXIOUS FOR PROMOTION.

I'M TERRIBLY THRILLED WITH MY NEW JOB.

WORK HARD, KAY, AND YOU'LL BE A BIG SUCCESS.

THANKS TO HER HARD WORK, KAY HAS LANDED A JOB AS A REPORTER ON A LARGE NATIONAL NEWSPAPER. THOUGH HER WORK IS EXACTING AND THE HOURS LONG AND UNCERTAIN, SHE IS EXTREMELY HAPPY IN HER CAREER.

I want to be a TRAVEL AGENT

BECAUSE SHE IS INTERESTED IN OTHER COUNTRIES AND GETS ON WELL WITH PEOPLE, BERYL IS GOING TO TRAIN TO BE A TRAVEL AGENT.

I LIKE THAT ONE BEST, MOTHER, BUT IT'S RATHER EXPENSIVE.

YOUR FATHER AND I WILL ADD TO YOUR SAVINGS AS A BIRTHDAY PRESENT.

BERYL HAS TAKEN A YEAR'S COURSE IN TYPING AND COMMERCIAL STUDIES AND HAS NOW OBTAINED THE POST OF JUNIOR IN A LOCAL TRAVEL AGENCY.

TWO FIRST CLASS RESERVATIONS TO NEW YORK? YES, MADAM, THAT WILL BE ARRANGED.

SHE HAS BEEN AT THE AGENCY FOR TWO YEARS. IN THAT TIME SHE HAS LEARNT ALL ABOUT PASSPORT REGULATIONS AND HOW TO COPE WITH THE VARIED REQUESTS OF CLIENTS. BERYL'S WORK IS NEVER DULL AND SHE IS QUICK TO LEARN. SHE EARNS THREE POUNDS TEN SHILLINGS A WEEK.

THERE, BERYL, WHAT DO YOU THINK OF MY EFFORT AT ADVERTISING?

I LIKE IT VERY MUCH, JOHN. IT'S CERTAINLY AN EYE-CATCHER!

TRAVEL AGENCIES RELY A GREAT DEAL ON THE CHARM AND ABILITY OF THEIR COUNTER PERSONNEL TO BOOST THEIR TOURS, ETC. BERYL ENJOYS EVERY MINUTE OF HER JOB, FROM PLANNING A LOCAL COACH TRIP TO ARRANGING A WORLD CRUISE.

I'VE ARRANGED LUNCH FOR YOU BOTH AT AN HOTEL.

OH, THANK YOU—WE'RE STARVING!

HER HOURS OF WORK ARE SOMETIMES IRREGULAR, FOR BERYL MAY HAVE TO MEET A CLIENT AT A STATION OR AIRPORT. HER TRAINING PERIOD IS FINISHED AND SHE NOW EARNS FIVE POUNDS A WEEK.

I AM HERE TO TELL YOU ABOUT OUR VARIOUS TOURS, SO PLEASE ASK AS MANY QUESTIONS AS YOU LIKE.

BERYL IS OFTEN ASKED TO TALK TO WOMEN'S CLUBS AND TO PLAN OUTINGS FOR THEM. HER WORK IS ABSORBING AND WHEN SHE HAS SAVED ENOUGH MONEY SHE HOPES TO GO ON A WORLD CRUISE HERSELF!

I want to be a Barrister

Sylvia has done brilliantly at school. She has a good voice and striking personality and hopes — though she knows how extremely difficult it is — to become a woman barrister.

THERE GOES MY APPLICATION, MOTHER. KEEP YOUR FINGERS CROSSED FOR ME.

I WILL— BUT DON'T EXPECT A REPLY STRAIGHT AWAY.

SHE HAS APPLIED FOR ENTRY TO AN INN OF COURT, OF WHICH THERE ARE FOUR. SCHOLARSHIP GRANTS ARE AVAILABLE, BUT A PAYMENT OF £200 MUST BE MADE ON JOINING. PART OF THIS IS RETURNABLE WHEN THE STUDENT IS CALLED TO THE BAR.

STUDENTS ARE REQUIRED TO DINE IN HALL AT LEAST SIX TIMES A TERM. EXAMINATIONS MAY BE SPACED OVER THREE YEARS AND ARE OF A VERY HIGH STANDARD. SUBJECTS INCLUDE CONSTITUTIONAL, CRIMINAL AND COMPANY LAW.

I CAN'T COME OUT TOMORROW NIGHT, SYLVIA.

WHAT A PITY! I'VE GOT TWO SPARE THEATRE TICKETS.

I'M NOT QUITE CLEAR ABOUT SOME OF THE DETAILS OF THIS CASE.

LET ME HAVE THE FILE AND I'LL RUN THROUGH THE MAIN ITEMS WITH YOU.

EXAMINATIONS PAST, SYLVIA NOW SPENDS A YEAR READING IN CHAMBERS. THIS COSTS A HUNDRED GUINEAS. IT IS NOT COMPULSORY, BUT NO BARRISTER CAN PRACTISE EFFECTIVELY WITHOUT IT. SYLVIA FINDS HER WORK COMPLETELY ABSORBING AND IS VERY HAPPY.

SYLVIA HAS BEEN NOMINATED BY A BENCHER OF HER INN AND CALLED TO THE BAR. SHE IS VERY CONSCIOUS OF HER GREAT PRIVILEGE AND SPENDS MOST OF HER SPARE TIME STUDYING AND LEARNING NEW LEGISLATIONS.

I HOPE TO BE ABLE TO GET NEARER HOME SOON AND BUILD UP A PRACTICE.

ALL THINGS CONSIDERED, I THINK I'D RATHER STAY IN LONDON.

... AND I RESPECTFULLY ASK YOU, M'LUD, TO ADJOURN THE CASE FOR FURTHER EVIDENCE.

BECAUSE OF HER BRILLIANT AND SYMPATHETIC HANDLING OF CASES, SYLVIA'S CLIENTS ARE INCREASING RAPIDLY. SHE NOW EARNS ABOUT A THOUSAND POUNDS A YEAR — BUT IT'S TAKEN HER TEN YEARS OF STUDY AND HARD WORK TO DO SO!

I want to be a Probation Officer

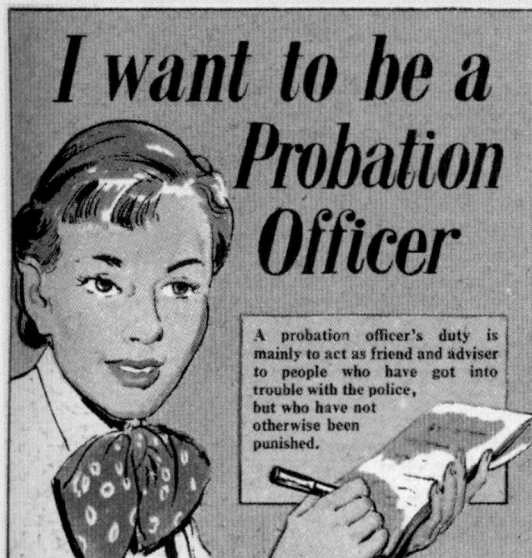

A probation officer's duty is mainly to act as friend and adviser to people who have got into trouble with the police, but who have not otherwise been punished.

HAVE YOU ENJOYED THE GARDEN PARTY, DADDY?

YES, MURIEL. I'M SO GLAD WE CAME.

MURIEL, WHO HAS DONE WELL IN HER G.C.E., HAS NOW MADE THE FIRST STEP TOWARDS ACHIEVING HER AMBITION BY SPENDING THREE YEARS AT A UNIVERSITY TAKING A DEGREE IN SOCIAL STUDIES. SOME LOCAL AUTHORITIES MAKE SPECIAL GRANTS TOWARDS THE COST OF FEES.

YOU'LL FIND SOME VERY INTERESTING CASES IN THAT FILE.

THANK YOU, MISS ELLIOT. I'LL STUDY THEM CAREFULLY.

NOW MURIEL HAS BEEN ACCEPTED FOR A YEAR'S TRAINING UNDER THE HOME OFFICE SCHEME. SHE STUDIES THE RECORDS OF PREVIOUS COURT CASES AND RECEIVES LECTURES ON MORAL WELFARE WORK, COURT PROCEDURE, AFTER-CARE AND MANY SOCIAL PROBLEMS.

I'VE JUST BEEN GIVEN MY FIRST APPOINTMENT.

SO HAVE I, MURIEL —AND I MUST SAY I'M FEELING RATHER NERVOUS.

PROBATION OFFICERS ARE APPOINTED BY JUSTICES OF THE PEACE AND MURIEL IS TO WORK NEAR HER HOME. SHE WILL RECEIVE £400 A YEAR AND THIS WILL BE INCREASED ANNUALLY TO A MAXIMUM OF £565.

JIMMY'S TURNED OVER A NEW LEAF SINCE YOU TOOK AN INTEREST IN HIM, MISS.

GOOD FOR YOU, JIMMY. KEEP IT UP.

AT FIRST MURIEL WORKS AMONG YOUNG OFFENDERS. SHE IS IN COURT WHEN THEY ARE PUT ON PROBATION AND SEES THEM FROM TIME TO TIME TO FIND OUT HOW THEY ARE GETTING ON.

ARE YOU GOING OFF DUTY NOW?

NO, I'VE STILL ANOTHER CALL TO MAKE.

MURIEL HAS BEEN A PROBATION OFFICER FOR FIVE YEARS NOW. HER JOB CALLS FOR GREAT TACT AND PATIENCE AND SOMETIMES THE HOURS ARE UNCERTAIN. BUT SHE LOVES HER WORK AND HER FIRM AND SYMPATHETIC GUIDANCE OF YOUNG OFFENDERS IS A GREAT ASSET TO THE COMMUNITY.

I want to be a Missionary

Janice, a keen member of her church, wants to work in Africa and hopes to train as a missionary when she has taken her G.C.E. and leaves school. Meanwhile, she reads all she can about the country she is going to live in, its history and its people.

SCHOOLDAYS OVER, JANICE HAS ENTERED A MISSIONARY TRAINING COLLEGE FOR TWO YEARS. THERE ARE NO FEES TO PAY, BUT JANICE IS TAUGHT ON THE UNDERSTANDING THAT SHE WILL WORK FOR THE SOCIETY WHEN HER TRAINING IS COMPLETE.

THIS IS JANICE WRIGHT. I KNOW YOU'LL DO ALL YOU CAN TO MAKE HER FEEL AT HOME.

HOW DO YOU DO?

MIND YOU WRITE AND TELL ME ALL ABOUT AFRICA WHEN YOU GET THERE.

HER TRAINING COMPLETE, JANICE IS VACCINATED AND INOCULATED AGAINST TYPHOID FEVER. ALTHOUGH A LITTLE SAD AT LEAVING HOME, SHE IS EAGERLY AWAITING THE LETTER FROM THE MISSIONARY SOCIETY TO TELL HER WHEN SHE CAN SAIL FOR AFRICA.

OF COURSE I WILL, DOCTOR WOOD. IT'S VERY NICE OF YOU TO TAKE SUCH AN INTEREST.

IT'S CHEERED MOTHER UP NO END TO KNOW THAT I'LL BE TRAVELLING WITH YOU AND YOUR WIFE.

YES, ALL THE WAY TO ZANZIBAR.

JANICE IS LUCKY ENOUGH TO BE GOING OUT WITH A DOCTOR AND HIS WIFE, RETURNING FROM LEAVE. SHE WILL RECEIVE ONLY A SMALL SALARY, BUT HER BOARD, LODGING AND PASSAGE HOME ARE PAID FOR BY THE MISSIONARY SOCIETY FOR WHICH SHE WORKS.

HAVING ARRIVED AT HER DESTINATION, JANICE IS TEACHING SMALL CHILDREN AND SETTLING DOWN QUICKLY INTO THE LIFE OF THE MISSION STATION WHERE SHE LIVES. WITH HER ARE FIVE OTHER EUROPEANS—TWO PRIESTS, A DOCTOR AND A NURSE.

ONE MORE ADDING-UP SUM AND THEN WE'LL HAVE SOME GAMES.

HELLO, JANICE. WHAT'S UP?

THIS LITTLE CHAP HAS CUT HIS FOOT.

SHE HAS BEEN ON THE STATION FOR TWO YEARS NOW AND IS DUE FOR SIX MONTHS' LEAVE SOON. SHE IS LOOKING FORWARD TO GOING HOME, BUT SHE WILL BE GLAD TO GET BACK TO HER AFRICAN BOYS AND GIRLS AGAIN, FOR SHE IS DOING THE SORT OF WORK THAT SHE HAS ALWAYS WANTED.

I want to be a Midwife

Because no girls are accepted for this profession before they are 20, Elizabeth has been filling in time since she left school. Now she is ready to begin her training at a midwifery hospital.

ELIZABETH SPENDS SOME OF HER TIME ATTENDING LECTURES. SHE RECEIVES HER TRAINING AND UNIFORM FREE AND £235 PER ANNUM, OF WHICH £108 IS DEDUCTED FOR BOARD, LODGING AND LAUNDRY. SHE FINDS HER WORK AMONG THE MOTHERS AND BABIES COMPLETELY ABSORBING.

... AND WHAT IS THE TERM FOR THAT PARTICULAR TEMPERATURE, NURSE WOOD?

INVERSE PYREXIA, SISTER.

RECREATIONAL FACILITIES IN ELIZABETH'S HOSPITAL ARE GOOD. THERE ARE TWO TENNIS COURTS, A TELEVISION ROOM, A DANCE HALL, GAMES ROOM AND A QUIET ROOM FOR STUDY.

THANKS, LIZ, THAT WAS A GOOD GAME. WHAT ABOUT ANOTHER ON WEDNESDAY?

I'LL LET YOU KNOW, MIKE. I'M NOT SURE YET WHAT TIME I'LL HAVE OFF.

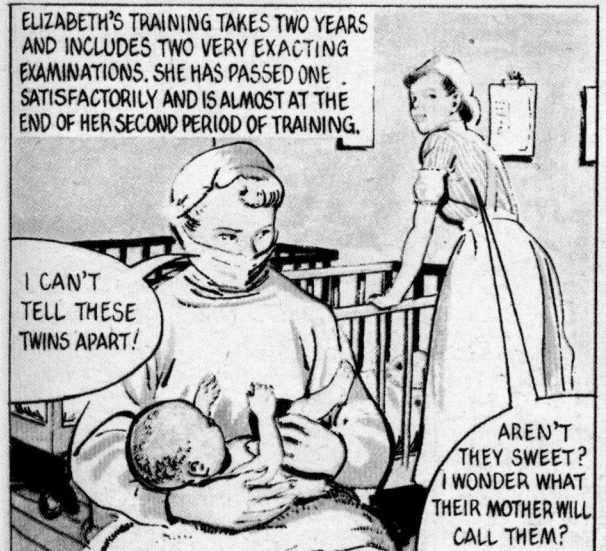

ELIZABETH'S TRAINING TAKES TWO YEARS AND INCLUDES TWO VERY EXACTING EXAMINATIONS. SHE HAS PASSED ONE SATISFACTORILY AND IS ALMOST AT THE END OF HER SECOND PERIOD OF TRAINING.

I CAN'T TELL THESE TWINS APART!

AREN'T THEY SWEET? I WONDER WHAT THEIR MOTHER WILL CALL THEM?

THE HOUSE WE'RE VISITING IS JUST OUTSIDE THE TOWN, ISN'T IT?

YES — ABOUT TWO MILES.

HALF OF ELIZABETH'S SECOND PERIOD OF TRAINING IS SPENT IN THE DISTRICT WORKING UNDER THE SUPERVISION OF A TRAINED MIDWIFE. THIS GIVES HER AN OPPORTUNITY OF MEETING ALL SORTS OF FAMILIES.

HER TRAINING COMPLETE, ELIZABETH IS NOW A DISTRICT MIDWIFE IN A SMALL TOWN. SHE SHARES A HOUSE WITH ANOTHER NURSE. HER SALARY IS NOW £395 A YEAR AND THIS WILL BE INCREASED ANNUALLY.

COME ALONG IN, MARGARET, AND SEE YOUR NEW BROTHER.

I want to be a STENO-TYPIST

ALICE WANTS TO BE A SECRETARY WHEN SHE LEAVES SCHOOL AND, BECAUSE SHE IS A MODERN YOUNG WOMAN, IS ANXIOUS TO LEARN BY THE MOST UP-TO-DATE METHODS.

I'D ADVISE STENOTYPING AS A CAREER FOR ALICE. MY NIECE LEARNT IT AND NOW HAS A VERY GOOD JOB.

THAT SOUNDS INTERESTING. WOULD YOU LIKE IT, ALICE?

A FRIEND TELLS ALICE AND HER MOTHER ABOUT SECRETARIAL COURSES WHICH INCLUDE STENOTYPING. THIS IS THE NAME FOR MACHINE SHORTHAND, IN WHICH SPEECH IS RECORDED IN PHONETIC SYLLABLES ON A BAND OF PAPER.

I DICTATED THAT PARAGRAPH AT ONE HUNDRED WORDS A MINUTE. LET'S HEAR HOW YOU TOOK IT DOWN, ALICE.

ALICE HAS DECIDED TO TAKE THE ADVICE OF HER MOTHER'S FRIEND AND IS NOW DOING A ONE-YEAR SECRETARIAL COURSE AT A COLLEGE TEACHING STENOTYPING. (THERE ARE SEVERAL OF THESE THROUGHOUT THE COUNTRY.) SHE ALSO LEARNS BOOK-KEEPING, ORDINARY TYPING AND GENERAL OFFICE ROUTINE.

WELL, HOW DID YOU GET ON, ALICE?

I WAS DREADFULLY NERVOUS AT FIRST, BUT AFTERWARDS IT WAS GREAT FUN.

SHE HAS NOW GAINED A HIGH STENOTYPING SPEED AS A SENIOR STUDENT AND IS ABLE TO GAIN EXPERIENCE BEFORE LOOKING FOR A JOB BY ASSISTING A VERBATIM REPORTER AT AN IMPORTANT CONFERENCE.

YOU DID YOUR TEST VERY WELL, MISS ADAMS, AND WE PROPOSE TO OFFER YOU A POST WITH THE FIRM.

THANK YOU. IT WILL BE A WONDERFUL OPPORTUNITY FOR ME.

ALICE HAS NOW GOT HER FIRST JOB WITH A LARGE FIRM OF IMPORTERS. IT WILL BE AN ORDINARY SECRETARIAL ONE AT FIRST, SO THAT SHE CAN GAIN CONFIDENCE AND EXPERIENCE. LATER, SHE HOPES TO USE HER HIGH SPEED STENOTYPING FOR COMMITTEE MEETINGS.

HAVE A GOOD TRIP, DARLING!

NOW AN EXPERIENCED SECRETARY, ALICE OFTEN GOES ABROAD WITH HER CHIEF TO RECORD BUSINESS DISCUSSIONS. HER STENOTYPING IS INVALUABLE AS IT IS ACCURATE, LEGIBLE AND ENABLES HER TO REPORT AT HIGH SPEED FOR LONG PERIODS. SHE EARNS £7 A WEEK.

I want to be a BANK CLERK

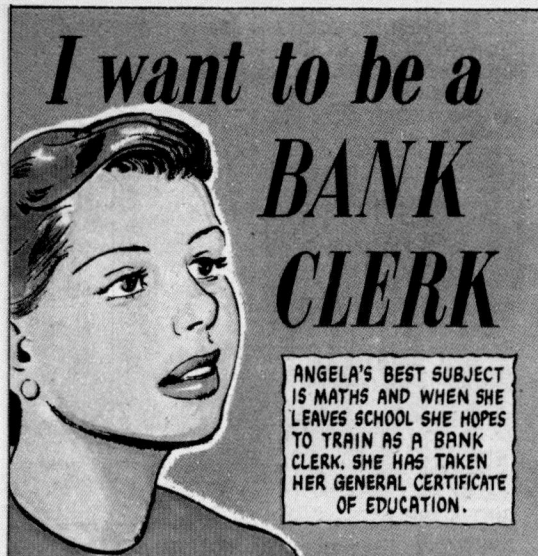

ANGELA'S BEST SUBJECT IS MATHS AND WHEN SHE LEAVES SCHOOL SHE HOPES TO TRAIN AS A BANK CLERK. SHE HAS TAKEN HER GENERAL CERTIFICATE OF EDUCATION.

HURRAH! MY APPLICATION HAS BEEN SUCCESSFUL AND I CAN START AT THE BANK ON MONDAY.

THAT'S WONDERFUL, DEAR. MAY I SEE WHAT THE MANAGER SAYS?

THE MAJORITY OF WOMEN EMPLOYED IN BANKS ARE MACHINE OPERATORS AND BOOK-KEEPERS, BUT THERE *ARE* VACANCIES FOR WOMEN CLERKS AND ANGELA HOPES EVENTUALLY TO BECOME ONE.

ANGELA, WHO HAS BEGUN HER CAREER AS A MACHINE OPERATOR, KNOWS THAT A KNOWLEDGE OF SHORT-HAND AND TYPING WILL BRING HER ADVANCEMENT AND A HIGHER SALARY, SO SHE IS TAKING A COURSE IN THIS AT HER LOCAL TECHNICAL SCHOOL.

MISS ROBSON'S A JOLLY GOOD TEACHER, ISN'T SHE?

YES. MY SHORT-HAND'S IMPROVED NO END SINCE SHE TOOK OVER

SHE HAS BEEN AT THE BANK FOR TWO YEARS NOW AND SHE HAS BEEN TAUGHT HOW TO USE THE MACHINES WHICH ELIMINATE THE NEED TO WRITE UP LEDGER ENTRIES BY HAND. HER SALARY IS ABOUT £200 A YEAR.

LET ME HAVE A COPY OF MRS SLOMAN'S ACCOUNT, WILL YOU?

RIGHT AWAY, MR DAVID.

MANY SOCIAL ACTIVITIES, SUCH AS MUSIC, OPERATIC AND DRAMATIC SOCIETIES, DANCES AND SPORTS CLUBS, ARE ARRANGED FOR BANK STAFFS AND ANGELA THOROUGHLY ENJOYS HER OFF-DUTY HOURS.

I HOPE THAT I DON'T FORGET MY LINES ON THE NIGHT!

YOU WON'T— BUT I'LL READ YOUR PART OVER WITH YOU AFTER REHEARSALS, IF YOU LIKE

AFTER A GOOD DEAL OF INTENSIVE TRAINING AND HARD WORK ANGELA HAS NOW BECOME A CASHIER IN HER LOCAL BANK. SHE EARNS ABOUT £300 A YEAR AND THIS WILL BE IN-CREASED ANNUALLY UP TO £400. SALARIES ARE HIGHER IN THE LONDON AREA.

HOW WILL YOU TAKE THE MONEY, MR WILLIAMS?

IN ONE POUND NOTES, PLEASE.

I want to be a Dancing Teacher

JUDY HAS BEEN ATTENDING CLASSES IN BALLET AND EURHYTHMICS SINCE SHE WAS QUITE SMALL AND IS KEEN TO TRAIN AS A TEACHER OF DANCING WHEN SHE LEAVES SCHOOL.

BE BACK PROMPTLY AT TWO O'CLOCK THIS AFTERNOON, EVERYBODY.

THANK GOODNESS IT'S LUNCHTIME. I COULD EAT A HORSE!

SHE HAS BEEN ACCEPTED AS A STUDENT BY A DANCING ACADEMY FOR AN INTENSIVE THREE-YEAR COURSE. STUDENTS MUST BE OVER 17 AND HAVE PASSED THEIR G.C.E. IN CERTAIN SUBJECTS. THE FEES ARE FAIRLY HIGH, BUT IN SOME CASES GRANTS ARE AVAILABLE.

RAISE YOUR ARM HIGHER, JUDY, THEN THE REST OF THE CLASS CAN TELL ME WHAT MUSCLES YOU ARE USING.

PART OF JUDY'S TRAINING INCLUDES LECTURES BY QUALIFIED PEOPLE ON ANATOMY AND PHYSIOLOGY. A KNOWLEDGE OF MUSCULAR CO-ORDINATION AND MOVEMENT WILL BE OF VALUE WHEN TEACHING BALLET POSITIONS AND DANCE ROUTINES.

I LOVED THAT SLOW MOVEMENT.

YES, AND THEY PLAYED IT SUPERBLY.

MUSIC APPRECIATION NATURALLY PLAYS A LARGE PART IN JUDY'S STUDIES. SHE IS TAUGHT HOW TO ADAPT TEMPO AND RHYTHM TO A PARTICULAR DANCE MOVEMENT AND, WHENEVER SHE CAN, SHE ATTENDS CONCERTS.

THAT WAS HEAPS BETTER. NOW LET'S TRY A SLOW FOXTROT. ALL RIGHT, MURIEL?

READY WHEN YOU ARE, JUDY.

NOW IN HER THIRD YEAR, JUDY HAS THE OPPORTUNITY OF TAKING CLASSES IN A NEARBY YOUTH CLUB. THIS HELPS TO PREPARE HER FOR THE TEACHING POST SHE HOPES TO OBTAIN LATER.

WHAT ARE OUR CHANCES IN THE FOLK DANCE FINALS THIS YEAR, JUDY?

I WON'T MAKE ANY RASH PROMISES, BUT THEY'VE IMPROVED A GOOD DEAL THIS TERM.

HAVING GAINED A WIDE KNOWLEDGE OF HER CHOSEN SUBJECT AND ITS BACK-GROUND, JUDY HAS OBTAINED A POST AS DANCING TEACHER AT A GIRLS' SCHOOL. ONE DAY, OF COURSE, SHE HOPES TO HAVE A DANCING SCHOOL OF HER OWN.

I want to be an Occupational Therapist

Keeping patients happy and interested during a long stay in hospital is part of the work of an Occupational Therapist. Monica hopes to become one.

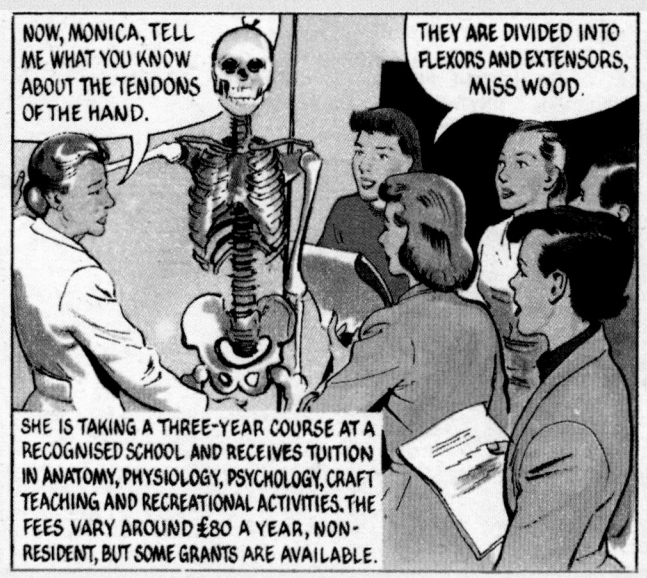

NOW, MONICA, TELL ME WHAT YOU KNOW ABOUT THE TENDONS OF THE HAND.

THEY ARE DIVIDED INTO FLEXORS AND EXTENSORS, MISS WOOD.

SHE IS TAKING A THREE-YEAR COURSE AT A RECOGNISED SCHOOL AND RECEIVES TUITION IN ANATOMY, PHYSIOLOGY, PSYCHOLOGY, CRAFT TEACHING AND RECREATIONAL ACTIVITIES. THE FEES VARY AROUND £80 A YEAR, NON-RESIDENT, BUT SOME GRANTS ARE AVAILABLE.

NOW IN HER THIRD YEAR, MONICA SPENDS MUCH OF HER TIME AT A HOSPITAL, BEING TRAINED BY AN EXPERIENCED THERAPIST AND WORKING WITH THE PATIENTS. SHE ALSO FINDS TIME FOR AMATEUR DRAMATICS, AS A KNOWLEDGE OF THIS WILL PROVE INVALUABLE TO HER.

I'M SORRY, JEAN. I KEEP FORGETTING THAT BIT.

NEVER MIND. JUST SAY IT ONCE MORE.

I'LL BE HOME IN ABOUT TWO HOURS' TIME, MOTHER.

COME ON, MONICA, THE TAXI'S WAITING TO TAKE US TO THE STATION.

HER TRAINING COMPLETE, MONICA IS HAVING A HOLIDAY BEFORE STARTING HER FIRST JOB. SHE IS TO BE ASSISTANT OCCUPATIONAL THERAPIST IN A HOSPITAL AT A SALARY OF £400 A YEAR, NON-RESIDENT.

YOU'RE GETTING ALONG WONDERFULLY. YOU OUGHT TO FINISH THAT SCARF BY THE WEEK-END.

IT'LL BE A NICE SURPRISE FOR MY WIFE.

MONICA HAS BEEN AT THE HOSPITAL FOR A YEAR NOW. THIS MAN HAS A LEG INJURY AND IS STRENGTHENING HIS MUSCLES BY WORKING THE TREADLE LOOM. MONICA WORKS FROM NINE O'CLOCK UNTIL FIVE-THIRTY.

WILL YOU BREAK OFF FOR A MOMENT, PLEASE. DOCTOR WANTS TO SEE YOU.

RIGHT-HO, MISS CARTER.

AFTER FIVE YEARS MONICA IS A SENIOR OCCUPATIONAL THERAPIST IN A GENERAL HOSPITAL. SHE HAS TWO ASSISTANTS AND RECEIVES £470 PER YEAR, OUT OF WHICH SHE PAYS FOR HER BOARD AND LODGING.

I want to be a Window-Dresser

Maureen's best subject is Art and she has a flair for display designing. When she leaves school she is going to train to become a store window-dresser.

"GOSH, I SHALL *DREAM* ABOUT CUTTING OUT PRICE TICKETS TONIGHT!"

"CHEER UP, MAUREEN. SALES-TIME ONLY COMES TWICE A YEAR."

MAUREEN HAS TAKEN A POST AS JUNIOR IN THE DISPLAY DEPARTMENT OF A LARGE STORE. SHE STARTS BY CUTTING OUT PRICE TICKETS AND LEARNING ABOUT THE 'PROPERTIES' USED IN WINDOW DISPLAY.

"MAY WE HAVE A DOZEN PAIRS OF BLACK SUEDE GLOVES FOR THE NORTH WINDOW?"

"NO, BUT I'VE GOT SOME PRETTY BLACK NYLON ONES THAT HAVE JUST COME IN."

NOW HELPING WITH ACTUAL WINDOW DISPLAYS, MAUREEN HAS TO DESCRIBE TO THE BUYERS OF THE VARIOUS DEPARTMENTS WHAT SHE WANTS TO SHOW. THEY SAY WHAT IS AVAILABLE, OR HAS A BETTER SELLING POWER.

"THAT BACKCLOTH IS AN ORIGINAL TOUCH, MOTHER. I MUST REMEMBER IT."

KEEN FOR PROMOTION, MAUREEN SPENDS A LOT OF TIME LOOKING AT THE WINDOW DISPLAYS OF OTHER STORES. SHE HAS BEEN WITH HER FIRM FOR TWO YEARS AND NOW EARNS £3.10.0. A WEEK.

"PAINTING THIS WALL IS HARD WORK."

"MMM, BUT IT LOOKS GOOD."

"HAND ME THAT POT OF VERMILION PLEASE, MAUREEN."

MAUREEN GOES TO NIGHT SCHOOL TWICE A WEEK FOR CLASSES IN COMMERCIAL DESIGN. SHE AND THE OTHER STUDENTS ARE PAINTING THE WALL DECORATIONS FOR A DANCE.

"THIS HAT DISPLAY IS VERY ATTRACTIVE, MAUREEN."

"GOOD, I'M GLAD YOU LIKE IT."

AFTER FIVE YEARS OF HARD WORK MAUREEN IS ALMOST AT THE TOP OF HER PROFESSION. SHE IS HEAD OF THE DISPLAY STAFF OF A LARGE STORE AND EARNS ABOUT £7.10.0. A WEEK.

I want to be a Dairy Worker

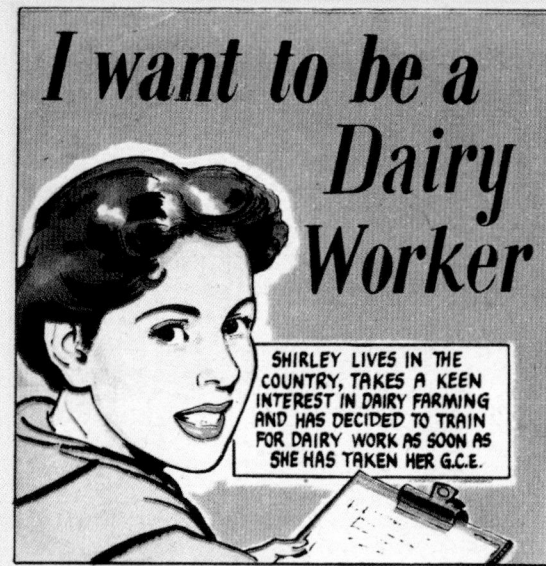

SHIRLEY LIVES IN THE COUNTRY, TAKES A KEEN INTEREST IN DAIRY FARMING AND HAS DECIDED TO TRAIN FOR DAIRY WORK AS SOON AS SHE HAS TAKEN HER G.C.E.

HAVING LEFT SCHOOL, SHIRLEY IS GOING TO TAKE A TWO-YEAR COURSE AT AN AGRICULTURAL COLLEGE. THERE ARE ALSO SHORTER COURSES IN DAIRYING AT FARM INSTITUTES, AS WELL AS DEGREE COURSES AT SOME UNIVERSITIES. MANY COUNTY COUNCILS OFFER SCHOLARSHIPS FOR THIS TRAINING.

BEFORE GOING TO THE AGRICULTURAL COLLEGE SHIRLEY MUST WORK FOR AT LEAST TWELVE MONTHS ON A DAIRY FARM. HERE SHE IS TAUGHT HOW TO LOOK AFTER THE STOCK AND EQUIPMENT, HOW TO MILK BY HAND AND WITH MACHINES, AND WILL HELP WITH THE MAKING OF BUTTER AND CHEESE. FOR THIS SHE MAY RECEIVE BOARD AND LODGING, AND LATER A SMALL SALARY.

NOW ON HER TWO-YEAR COURSE AT THE COLLEGE, SHIRLEY RECEIVES TUITION IN CHEMISTRY AND BACTERIOLOGY, AS WELL AS THE PRACTICAL SIDE OF DAIRY WORK. SHE WILL TAKE THE EXAMINATIONS, BOTH WRITTEN AND ORAL, IN SIX SUBJECTS AT THE END OF HER COURSE.

HER TRAINING COMPLETED, SHIRLEY HAS NOW QUALIFIED FOR HER DIPLOMA IN DAIRYING. SHE HAS A SHORT HOLIDAY BEFORE TAKING HER FIRST POST AS ASSISTANT HERDSWOMAN ON A LARGE FARM. SHE WILL BEGIN AT ABOUT £250 A YEAR.

DAIRYING FORMS A VERY IMPORTANT PART OF FARMING TODAY AND AS A HERDSWOMAN SHIRLEY HOLDS A RESPONSIBLE JOB. SHE HAS BEEN AT THE FARM FIVE YEARS NOW AND IS VERY HAPPY. HER SALARY HAS RISEN TO OVER £350 A YEAR.

I want to be a Chiropodist

Chiropody is the treatment of the feet, toe-nails, etc., and Jane is going to take a 3-year course of training in this. She has a good knowledge of chemistry and physics, which is essential, and has taken her G.C.E.

SHE LIVES IN A STUDENTS' HOSTEL AND ATTENDS THE SCHOOL OF CHIROPODY DAILY FOR LECTURES AND DEMONSTRATIONS. THE FEES ARE BETWEEN 30 AND 40 GUINEAS A YEAR FOR THE THREE-YEAR COURSE AND JANE WILL TAKE AN EXAMINATION AT THE END OF EACH YEAR.

COME AND HAVE COFFEE WITH ME AFTER THIS LECTURE, LIZ?

RIGHT-HO, JANE.

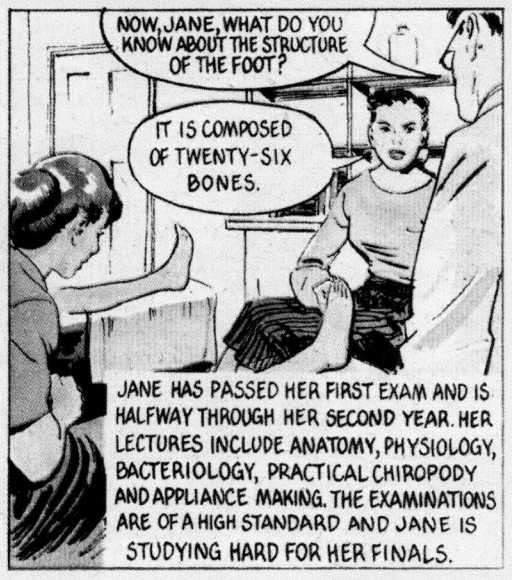

NOW, JANE, WHAT DO YOU KNOW ABOUT THE STRUCTURE OF THE FOOT?

IT IS COMPOSED OF TWENTY-SIX BONES.

JANE HAS PASSED HER FIRST EXAM AND IS HALFWAY THROUGH HER SECOND YEAR. HER LECTURES INCLUDE ANATOMY, PHYSIOLOGY, BACTERIOLOGY, PRACTICAL CHIROPODY AND APPLIANCE MAKING. THE EXAMINATIONS ARE OF A HIGH STANDARD AND JANE IS STUDYING HARD FOR HER FINALS.

GOOD-BYE, JANE. DON'T FORGET TO COME AND SEE US WHEN YOU ARE IN LONDON.

I WON'T— AND THANK YOU FOR ALL YOU'VE TAUGHT ME.

SHE HAS PASSED HER FINALS AND HAS BEEN ACCEPTED AS A MEMBER OF THE SOCIETY OF CHIROPODISTS. SHE IS NOW ENTITLED TO REGISTER WITH THE BOARD OF REGISTRATION OF MEDICAL AUXILIARIES, WHICH IS RECOGNISED BY THE MEDICAL PROFESSION.

MRS REYNOLDS, WILL YOU COME IN NOW PLEASE?

JANE SOMEWHAT NERVOUSLY BEGINS HER FIRST JOB AS ASSISTANT CHIROPODIST IN A LOCAL FOOT CLINIC. SHE WORKS A SEVEN-HOUR DAY WITH FREE WEEK-ENDS AND STARTS AT A SALARY OF £7 A WEEK, NON-RESIDENT.

THERE, JANE, HOW DOES THAT LOOK?

WONDERFUL, DADDY. THANK YOU VERY MUCH.

J. UPTON MChS

BY CAREFUL SAVING AFTER FOUR YEARS JANE HAS MANAGED TO EQUIP HERSELF FOR PRIVATE PRACTICE. SHE WORKS PART-TIME IN THE LOCAL FOOT CLINIC AND FITS IN HER APPOINTMENTS IN THE AFTERNOON. SHE HOPES TO INCREASE HER CLIENTELE IN TIME, SO THAT SHE CAN EARN HER LIVING BY HER OWN EFFORTS.

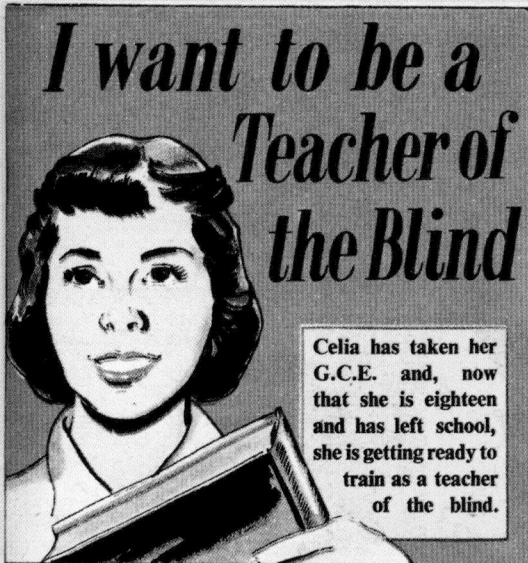

I want to be a Teacher of the Blind

Celia has taken her G.C.E. and, now that she is eighteen and has left school, she is getting ready to train as a teacher of the blind.

ARE YOU COMING DOWN TO SUPPER NOW, CELIA?

THE CAREER SHE'S CHOSEN IS A SPECIALISED ONE AND CELIA IS TAKING A TWO-YEAR COURSE AT A COLLEGE FOR TEACHERS OF THE BLIND. SHE IS A RESIDENT STUDENT AND PART OF HER FEES ARE PAID BY A LOCAL GRANT.

YES, I'VE JUST GOT THIS PAGE TO FINISH AND THEN I'LL BE WITH YOU.

THAT'S A GOOD ATTEMPT, CELIA. NOW YOU CAN TRY SOMETHING BIGGER.

THANK YOU, MISS DALTON, THAT SHOULD BE INTERESTING.

AS WELL AS A KNOWLEDGE OF BRAILLE AND THE PEG AND BOARD SYSTEM FOR TEACHING ARITHMETIC TO BLIND CHILDREN, CELIA ALSO LEARNS HANDICRAFT. SHE IS HALFWAY THROUGH HER SECOND YEAR AND HOPES TO TAKE HER DIPLOMA AT THE END OF THE TERM.

CELIA HAS WORKED HARD AT HER STUDIES AND HAS OBTAINED HER COVETED DIPLOMA, WHICH IS RECOGNISED BY THE MINISTRY OF EDUCATION. SHE IS HAVING A SHORT HOLIDAY BEFORE TAKING UP HER FIRST JOB.

DON'T OVERDO IT, OR YOU'LL HAVE SUN-STOKE INSTEAD.

I SHALL GO BACK AS BROWN AS A BERRY WITH THIS MARVELLOUS WEATHER.

NOW WHOSE TURN IS IT TO BE GOLDILOCKS TODAY?

IT'S MINE, MISS.

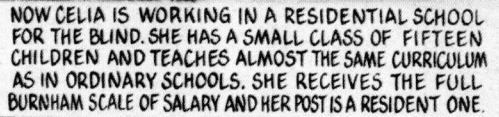

NOW CELIA IS WORKING IN A RESIDENTIAL SCHOOL FOR THE BLIND. SHE HAS A SMALL CLASS OF FIFTEEN CHILDREN AND TEACHES ALMOST THE SAME CURRICULUM AS IN ORDINARY SCHOOLS. SHE RECEIVES THE FULL BURNHAM SCALE OF SALARY AND HER POST IS A RESIDENT ONE.

WISH I COULD PLAY A VIOLIN LIKE THAT.

IT WAS SUPERB, WASN'T IT?

ONE OF HER MOST ENJOYABLE DUTIES IS ESCORTING SOME OF THE OLDER PUPILS TO CONCERTS. BLIND CHILDREN ARE GIVEN EVERY ENCOURAGEMENT IN THESE SPECIAL SCHOOLS TO TAKE A FULL SHARE IN SOCIAL LIFE. CELIA HAS FOUND HAPPINESS IN A THOROUGHLY WORTHWHILE JOB.

I BET HE PRACTISES ABOUT EIGHT HOURS A DAY.

I want to be a Demonstrator

LOIS IS KEEN ON HOUSECRAFT. WHEN SHE HAS TAKEN HER G.C.E. SHE IS GOING TO TRAIN AS A DEMONSTRATOR OF DOMESTIC APPLIANCES.

SHE IS TAKING A TWO-YEAR COURSE IN DOMESTIC SCIENCE AT A TRAINING SCHOOL NEAR HER HOME, AND A DIPLOMA IN THIS SUBJECT IS ESSENTIAL TO HER CAREER. THERE ARE A NUMBER OF THESE SCHOOLS THROUGHOUT THE COUNTRY.

I DON'T THINK THE CAKES ARE QUITE DONE YET, DO YOU, MARY?

THEY LOOK ALL RIGHT TO ME.

LOIS HAS NOW OBTAINED HER DIPLOMA AND IS TO BEGIN AS A 'JUNIOR' IN HER LOCAL GAS INDUSTRY SHOWROOMS. SHE WILL SERVE A SIX MONTHS' PROBATIONARY PERIOD AT A SALARY OF ABOUT £350.

YOU WILL JOIN US ON MONDAY, THEN.

YES, MISS JENKINS, I'M LOOKING FORWARD TO IT.

NUTLEY ROAD IS JUST ALONG ON THE RIGHT, MISS.

THANK YOU FOR DIRECTING ME.

PART OF LOIS'S JOB CONSISTS OF VISITING YOUNG WIVES ON THE NEW HOUSING ESTATES AND SHOWING THEM HOW TO USE THEIR GAS STOVES, REFRIGERATORS, ETC.

NOW IN HER SECOND YEAR, LOIS SPENDS A LOT OF HER TIME GIVING COOKERY DEMONSTRATIONS AND RECEIVES £450 A YEAR. SHE HAS TAKEN A COURSE OF ELOCUTION TO HELP HER WITH PUBLIC SPEAKING.

... AND SO YOU CAN SEE FOR YOUR-SELVES, LADIES, THE GOOD POINTS OF THIS PAR-TICULAR TYPE OF COOKER.

AFTER SEVERAL YEARS LOIS HAS NOW BEEN APPOINTED SENIOR HOME SERVICE ADVISER AND RECEIVES ABOUT £550 A YEAR. SHE COVERS A WIDE AREA AND HAS THE USE OF A CAR TO TRAVEL AROUND IN.

GOOD-BYE, DEAR. WILL YOU BE BACK FOR LUNCH?

NO, MOTHER, I'LL BE HOME ABOUT SIX.

I want to be an Optician

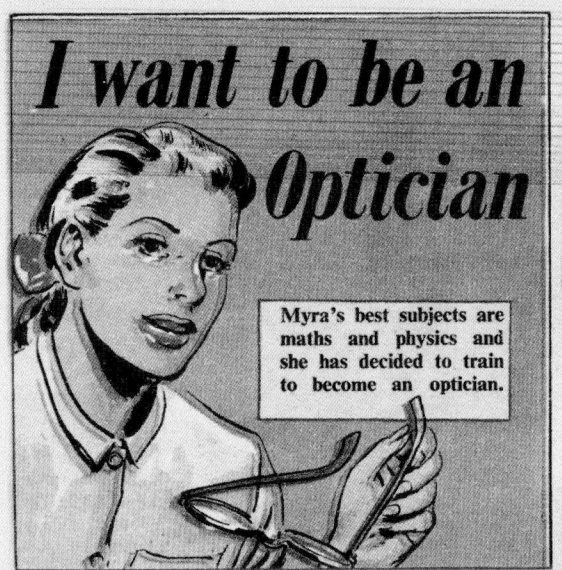

Myra's best subjects are maths and physics and she has decided to train to become an optician.

HAVING TAKEN HER G.C.E., MYRA IS NOW PREPARING FOR THE QUALIFYING EXAMINATION OF THE BRITISH OPTICAL ASSOCIATION. THE COURSE LASTS THREE YEARS AND MYRA IS LUCKY TO BE STAYING IN LONDON WITH HER AUNT FOR THIS TIME.

HELLO, DEAR, IT IS NICE TO SEE YOU AGAIN.

HELLO, AUNT MARY. I HOPE YOU HAVEN'T BEEN WAITING LONG.

NOW, MISS WETHERALL, LOOK INTO THE EYE THROUGH THIS AND TELL ME WHAT YOU SEE.

YES, SIR.

PART OF MYRA'S TRAINING CONSISTS OF LEARNING ABOUT THE PHYSIOLOGY OF THE EYE. MOST TECHNICAL COLLEGES IN THE LARGER TOWNS OFFER A COURSE IN OPTHALMICS. MYRA'S FEES ARE THIRTY POUNDS A YEAR, NON-RESIDENT, AND THE FEES FOR THE WHOLE EXAMINATION ARE ABOUT £23. THERE ARE SOME GRANTS AVAILABLE.

TO MYRA, THE FIRST WOMAN OPTICIAN IN THE FAMILY!

CONGRATULATIONS, MYRA.

THANK YOU VERY MUCH, EVERYONE.

BY A COINCIDENCE, MYRA CELEBRATES HER 21st BIRTHDAY ON THE SAME DAY THAT SHE PASSES HER QUALIFYING EXAM. SHE HAS STUDIED HARD FOR THREE YEARS AND INTENDS TO WORK FOR A FURTHER PERIOD UNDER A QUALIFIED OPTICIAN IN ORDER TO GET HER F.B.O.A. DIPLOMA.

MYRA HAS ACHIEVED HER DIPLOMA AND IS CONTINUING TO WORK FOR THE OPTICIAN WHO TRAINED HER. SHE RECEIVES £350 A YEAR AND THIS AMOUNT IS INCREASED YEARLY UP TO £500.

I WONDERED IF MY SPECTACLES HAVE ARRIVED YET.

YES, THEY CAME YESTERDAY. WILL YOU SIT DOWN FOR A MOMENT, PLEASE?

THERE YOU ARE, MYRA, YOUR NAME ON THE DOOR AT LAST. HOW DOES IT LOOK?

IT LOOKS WONDERFUL TO ME.

AFTER ANOTHER FIVE YEARS' HARD WORK, MYRA HAS GONE INTO PARTNERSHIP WITH A FELLOW OPTICIAN AND TOGETHER THEY HAVE OPENED A SHOP IN THEIR HOME TOWN. MYRA IS HAPPY IN HER WORK, KNOWING THAT HER JOB IS THOROUGHLY WORTHWHILE.

I want to be a Radio Technician

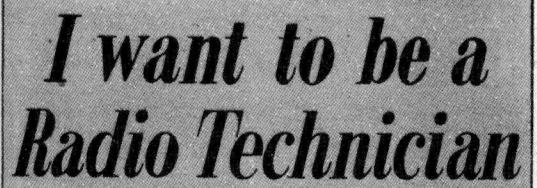

ANITA HAS CHOSEN AN UNUSUAL AND DIFFICULT JOB. SHE HAS MADE A COMPLETE STUDY OF PHYSICS AND MATHEMATICS AND, WHEN SHE IS EIGHTEEN, HOPES TO TRAIN AS A RADIO TECHNICIAN.

ANITA IS TAKING A THREE-YEAR COURSE AT A TECHNICAL COLLEGE. HER FEES ARE ABOUT £100 A YEAR AND THE TRAINING WILL ENABLE HER TO SIT FOR THE CITY AND GUILDS OF LONDON INSTITUTE EXAMINATION.

WILL YOU LEND ME YOUR NOTES ON THAT RADAR LECTURE, JOHN? I MISSED THE FIRST HALF HOUR.

THIS IS THE RADIO RECEIVING ROOM AND HERE YOU SEE ONE OF OUR MEN HELPING TO PLOT AN AIRCRAFT'S COURSE.

KEEN TO LEARN ALL SHE CAN ABOUT HER WORK, ANITA TAKES FULL ADVANTAGE OF THE INVITATIONS THAT THE STUDENTS RECEIVE TO MAKE TOURS OF RADIO STATIONS. SHE IS HALFWAY THROUGH HER SECOND YEAR AND STUDYING HARD FOR HER FINAL EXAMS.

I MUST GO IN ANOTHER TEN MINUTES. I'VE AN ESSAY TO FINISH TONIGHT.

ALL RIGHT—BUT WE MUST HAVE A RETURN GAME LATER.

RECREATIONAL FACILITIES IN ANITA'S COLLEGE ARE GOOD AND SHE MAKES THE MOST OF HER FREE TIME. AFTER SHE HAS PASSED HER FINAL EXAMS SHE MAY EITHER TAKE A POST IN RADIO ENGINEERING OR SPECIALISE IN A PARTICULAR BRANCH FOR WHICH SHE WILL NEED FURTHER STUDY.

ANITA HAS COMPLETED HER THREE-YEAR COURSE, OBTAINED HER RADIO CERTIFICATE AND, IN A PROFESSION WHICH HAS VERY FEW VACANCIES FOR WOMEN, FOUND A JOB WITH A LOCAL RADIO ENGINEERING FIRM. HER SALARY WILL BE £250 A YEAR FOR THE FIRST SIX MONTHS.

YOU CAN START WITH US ON MONDAY THEN, MISS EDGE?

YES. I SHALL LOOK FORWARD TO IT VERY MUCH.

THAT SUPPRESSOR IS A DEFINITE IMPROVEMENT ON THE OLD TYPE.

IT'S TAKEN THREE MONTHS' TRIAL AND ERROR TO GET IT TO THAT STAGE.

AFTER FIVE YEARS OF HARD WORK, SPENDING SOME TIME IN EACH DEPARTMENT OF HER FIRM, ANITA HAS BEEN APPOINTED ASSISTANT TO THE HEAD OF RESEARCH. SHE SPECIALISES IN RADIO AND TELE-VISION WORK AND RECEIVES £500 A YEAR

I want to be a Plastics Designer

Ruby likes working with her hands and is good at modelling. When she has taken her G.C.E. she is going to train to be a Plastics Designer.

SHE IS TAKING A YEAR'S COURSE IN DESIGN AT HER LOCAL ART SCHOOL AND HOPES TO OBTAIN A DIPLOMA IN PLASTICS BY TAKING THE TWO EXAMINATIONS SET BY THE CITY AND GUILDS OF LONDON INSTITUTE. THE COST OF THE YEAR'S TRAINING IS ABOUT £30.

DESIGNED YOUR PRIZE-WINNING LAMP SHADE YET, TONY?

NOT YET, BUT IT'S COMING ON.

WHAT ABOUT DESIGNING ME A PLASTIC RUGGER BALL, SIS?

YOU'D BE SURPRISED JUST WHAT *CAN* BE DONE WITH PLASTICS THESE DAYS, DON!

AFTER WORKING HARD ALL THE WEEK, RUBY RELAXES AT A RUGBY MATCH WITH HER BROTHER. SHE HAS COMPLETED HER COURSE IN DESIGN AND IS TAKING A POST IN A LARGE PLASTICS FIRM WHERE SHE WILL LEARN THE TECHNICAL SIDE OF HER JOB.

COULD I BE GIVEN A TRANSFER TO THE POLISHING SECTION, MISS HORN?

YES, YOU SEEM TO HAVE GOT THE HANG OF MOULDING, RUBY.

PLASTICS ARE USED FOR MANY DIFFERENT PURPOSES. RUBY IS FASCINATED BY THE VARIETY OF JOBS THERE ARE IN THE INDUSTRY AND IS LEARNING ALL SHE CAN. SHE RECEIVES THREE POUNDS A WEEK WHILE TRAINING.

AFTER TWO YEARS LEARNING ALL ABOUT THE PRODUCTION OF PLASTICS, RUBY NOW CONCENTRATES ENTIRELY ON DESIGN. THERE ARE TWO OTHER DESIGNERS IN HER DEPARTMENT AND, AS THE JUNIOR, SHE RECEIVES FIVE POUNDS A WEEK.

THAT SORT OF KITCHEN EQUIPMENT ALWAYS SELLS WELL.

YES, I THINK IT HAS DEFINITE POSSIBILITIES.

WITH HER ADDED EXPERIENCE IN THE INDUSTRY, RUBY HAS PASSED THE CITY AND GUILDS EXAMINATIONS AND OBTAINED A DIPLOMA IN PLASTICS. SHE FINDS A SATISFYING OUTLET FOR HER CREATIVE ABILITY AND IS EXTREMELY HAPPY IN HER JOB.

I'M LONGING TO KNOW WHAT YOU THINK OF MY LATEST HANDBAG DESIGN, DADDY.

YOU'RE A LUCKY GIRL TO HAVE IT EXHIBITED LIKE THIS.

I want to be a Dental Nurse

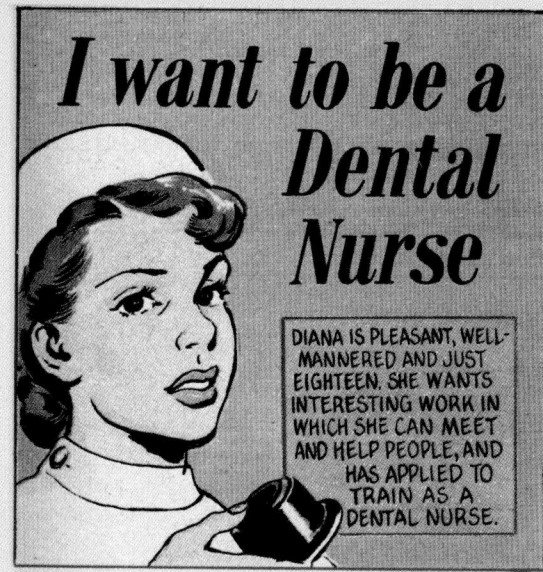

DIANA IS PLEASANT, WELL-MANNERED AND JUST EIGHTEEN. SHE WANTS INTERESTING WORK IN WHICH SHE CAN MEET AND HELP PEOPLE, AND HAS APPLIED TO TRAIN AS A DENTAL NURSE.

OH, JOLLY GOOD. THEY SAY I CAN START NEXT TERM.

THAT'S FINE, BUT YOU WILL HAVE TO WORK HARD.

COMPETITION FOR PLACES IN TRAINING COURSES IS KEEN AND A GOOD EDUCATION IS ESSENTIAL. DIANA WILL TRAIN AT A HOSPITAL FOR TWELVE MONTHS, BUT COULD QUALIFY BY WORKING FOR TWO YEARS WITH A DENTIST (OR AT A SCHOOL DENTAL CLINIC) AND PASSING THE DENTAL NURSES AND ASSISTANTS EXAMINATION.

AT FIRST SHE RECEIVES ABOUT £2 A WEEK, BUT WILL GET A LITTLE MORE WHEN SHE PASSES THE FIRST EXAMINATION. SHE STUDIES ANATOMY, PHYSIOLOGY, NURSING, ANAESTHETICS, RADIO-GRAPHY AND X-RAY DEVELOPING.

YOU KNOW THAT THE OUTER COVERING OF THE TOOTH IS CALLED ENAMEL. NOW WHAT IS *THIS*?

THAT IS CALLED THE DENTINE.

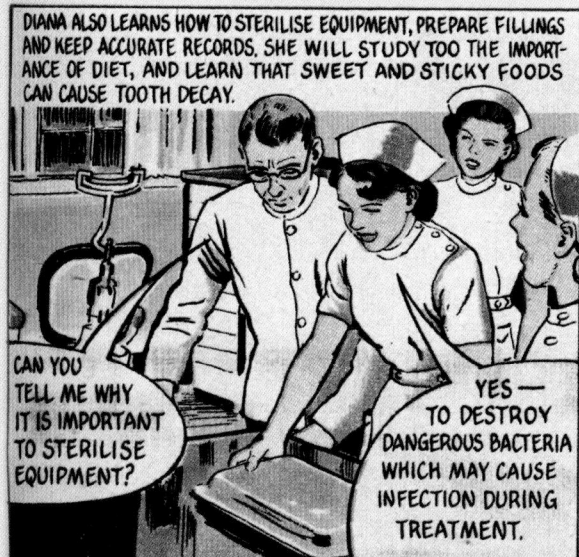

DIANA ALSO LEARNS HOW TO STERILISE EQUIPMENT, PREPARE FILLINGS AND KEEP ACCURATE RECORDS. SHE WILL STUDY TOO THE IMPORT-ANCE OF DIET, AND LEARN THAT SWEET AND STICKY FOODS CAN CAUSE TOOTH DECAY.

CAN YOU TELL ME WHY IT IS IMPORTANT TO STERILISE EQUIPMENT?

YES — TO DESTROY DANGEROUS BACTERIA WHICH MAY CAUSE INFECTION DURING TREATMENT.

YOU WILL BE ABLE TO HELP ME A LOT.

I HOPE SO. I HAVE HAD A THOROUGH TRAINING.

NOW FULLY TRAINED, DIANA HAS JOINED THE BRITISH DENTAL NURSES SOCIETY WHICH HAS ITS OWN UNIFORM, INSURANCE SCHEME, EMPLOYMENT REGISTER AND MAG-AZINE. SHE HAS APPLIED FOR HER FIRST JOB AND HAS BEEN ACCEPTED.

HERE IS MRS LLOYD'S X-RAY.

GOOD. WILL YOU MIX AN AMALGAM FILLING, PLEASE?

SALARIES DEPEND ON THE EMPLOYER, BUT THEY ARE UNLIKELY TO BE LESS THAN £300 A YEAR. DIANA WORKS CLOSELY WITH THE DENTIST AND GOES WITH HIM WHEN HE PRACTISES AT HOSPITALS AND NURSING HOMES.

I want to be a Dancer

LINDA HAS HAD DANCING LESSONS SINCE SHE WAS QUITE SMALL AND, NOW THAT SHE HAS LEFT SCHOOL, SHE IS GOING TO TRAIN TO BECOME A PROFESSIONAL.

HAVING APPLIED TO A SCHOOL OF DANCING, LINDA HAS HAD AN AUDITION AND BEEN ACCEPTED FOR TRAINING. SHE WILL TAKE A THREE-YEAR COURSE THERE AND, DURING THAT TIME, SEVERAL EXAMINATIONS. COSTS VARY ACCORDING TO THE SCHOOL. EXAMINATION FEES ARE EXTRA.

YOU'LL START WITH US NEXT TERM THEN, LINDA.

THANK YOU. I'M SO PLEASED I'VE BEEN ACCEPTED.

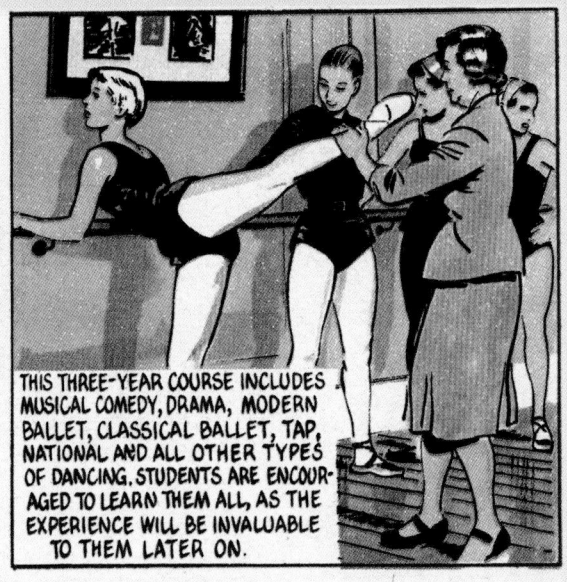

THIS THREE-YEAR COURSE INCLUDES MUSICAL COMEDY, DRAMA, MODERN BALLET, CLASSICAL BALLET, TAP, NATIONAL AND ALL OTHER TYPES OF DANCING. STUDENTS ARE ENCOURAGED TO LEARN THEM ALL, AS THE EXPERIENCE WILL BE INVALUABLE TO THEM LATER ON.

I'VE PASSED, MOTHER! I'VE PASSED!

AT THE END OF HER TRAINING LINDA HAS TAKEN AND PASSED HER FINAL EXAMINATION SHE WILL NOW START LOOKING FOR HER FIRST PROFESSIONAL ENGAGEMENT.

THAT GIRL'S NOT BAD.

LET'S TRY HER OUT IN THE NEW SHOW.

LINDA'S AMBITION IS TO DANCE IN A MUSICAL SHOW BECAUSE SHE IS KEEN ON MODERN BALLET AND KNOWS SHE IS GOOD AT IT. SHE HAS APPLIED FOR A PART IN ONE AND IS BEING AUDITIONED SO THAT THE PRODUCERS CAN DECIDE WHETHER OR NOT SHE IS GOOD ENOUGH TO BE TAKEN ON.

SHE HAS BEEN ACCEPTED FOR THE CHORUS AND LATER ON HOPES TO GET BIGGER PARTS. THOUGH LINDA REALIZES THAT THIS MAY NOT HAPPEN QUICKLY, SHE LOVES DANCING AND FEELS THAT THE PATIENCE AND HARD WORK REQUIRED OF HER WILL BE WELL WORTH WHILE.

AT LAST— LINDA'S FIRST PART!

IT'S A SMALL ONE, BUT IT'S A START.

Concerning YOU

Going Abroad

A LONG JOURNEY IS VERY TIRING, SO GO TO BED EARLY THE NIGHT BEFORE. TEN HOURS SLEEP SHOULD BE YOUR TARGET.

DON'T TRAVEL IN YOUR BEST CLOTHES. THE AMOUNT OF DUST AND CINDERS THAT COLLECT ON ONE'S PERSON IS FANTASTIC. AIM AT BEING NEAT, BUT COMFORTABLE.

ONCE THE CHANNEL IS CROSSE ABANDON ALL THOUGHTS OF WAS UNTIL THE JOURNEY IS OVER. PA A SOAPY FACE-FLANNEL AND MOIST SPONGE, AND USE THESE FRESHEN YOUR HANDS. TAKE CLEANSING PADS FOR FACE AN NECK AND, IF ANY WATER IS AVAI USE IT FOR CLEANING YOUR TEETH ZEN COLOGNE WILL KEEP YOU COOL

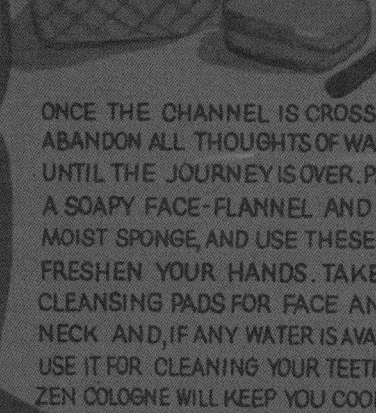

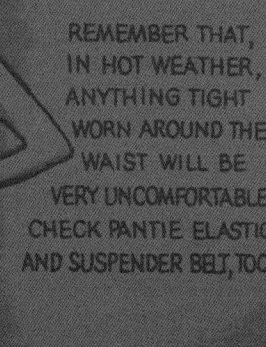

REMEMBER THAT, IN HOT WEATHER, ANYTHING TIGHT WORN AROUND THE WAIST WILL BE VERY UNCOMFORTABLE. CHECK PANTIE ELASTIC AND SUSPENDER BELT, TOO

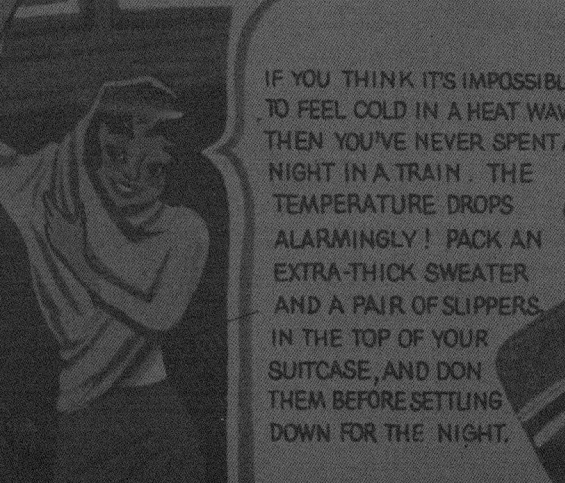

IF YOU THINK IT'S IMPOSSIBLE TO FEEL COLD IN A HEAT WAVE, THEN YOU'VE NEVER SPENT A NIGHT IN A TRAIN. THE TEMPERATURE DROPS ALARMINGLY! PACK AN EXTRA-THICK SWEATER AND A PAIR OF SLIPPERS IN THE TOP OF YOUR SUITCASE, AND DON THEM BEFORE SETTLING DOWN FOR THE NIGHT.

NO WHISTLE-BLAST SIGNALS THE DEPARTUI OF TRAINS ABROAD, THE SIMPLY DRAW OUT ON TIME SO MAKE SURE THAT YOU'F IN YOUR SEAT EARLY. TAK A FLASK OF COFFEE OR DILUT FRUIT-JUICE WITH YOU. THI THINGS BOUGHT ON STATIC CAN RUN AWAY WITH YI FOREIGN CURRENC

3

Concerning You:
Correct Behaviour for
Every Situation

Concerning YOU

Invitation

Your First Dance

MANY OF YOU WILL BE GOING TO YOUR FIRST DANCE THIS CHRISTMAS. THAT IS A MILESTONE IN EVERYBODY'S LIFE AND CALLS FOR SPECIAL PREPARATIONS. WEAR A LONG, OR SHORT DRESS, WHICHEVER YOU PREFER.

BUT IT MUST HAVE A FULL SKIRT — NO EXCEPTIONS TO THIS RULE. IF YOU HANKER AFTER A SLINKY CREATION WITH A TRAIN, JUST PICTURE YOURSELF TRYING TO DANCE THE GAY GORDONS IN IT!

YOUR HANDS WILL BE ON DISPLAY, SO MANICURE THEM THE NIGHT BEFORE. IF THEY HAVE BEEN NEGLECTED AND THERE IS NO TIME TO IMPROVE THEM, WHY NOT WEAR GLOVES?

HAIR MUST BE EXTRA WELL-GROOMED. SHAMPOO A DAY OR TWO BEFORE AND FOLLOW UP BY VIGOROUS BRUSHING. A TRACE OF CREAM BRILLIANTINE ON THE NIGHT WORKS WONDERS.

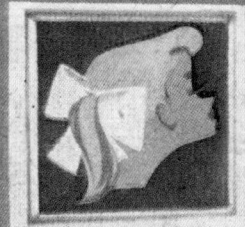

IF YOU DO YOUR HAIR IN A PONY-TAIL, TIE IT WITH A GENEROUS BOW OF SATIN RIBBON. OR MAKE A WREATH OF TINY ARTIFICIAL FLOWERS AND ENCIRCLE THE 'TAIL' WITH IT.

A SHOULDER LENGTH BOB (SEE BELOW) LOOKS PRETTY BRUSHED BACK AND HELD WITH A BAND OF INCH-WIDE VELVET RIBBON, ALICE-FASHION.

SOME OF YOU WILL BE OLD ENOUGH FOR MAKE-UP. EXCITEMENT WILL GIVE YOU COLOUR AND MAKE YOUR EYES SPARKLE, SO LESS OF THIS WILL BE NECESSARY THAN YOU THINK. A DUSTING OF POWDER OVER A LIGHT FOUNDATION, A PALE ROSE LIPSTICK, AND LASHES AND BROWS GROOMED WITH A LITTLE BRILLIANTINE IS ALL YOU NEED.

NEXT, DEPORTMENT. DON'T BE FOREVER CHECKING ON THE SEAMS OF YOUR STOCKINGS. SEE THAT SHOULDER STRAPS ARE PINNED OUT OF SIGHT. FINALLY, FORGET ALL ABOUT YOUR APPEARANCE, AND ENJOY THE FUN!

Concerning YOU

CHRISTMAS PARTY

IF YOU ARE PLAYING HOSTESS AT A CHRISTMAS PARTY THIS YEAR, HERE ARE A FEW SUGGESTIONS TO HELP MAKE THE EVENING A SUCCESS.

BE READY HALF AN HOUR BEFORE YOU EXPECT YOUR FIRST GUEST. ONCE YOUR PERSONAL PREPARATIONS ARE COMPLETED, FORGET ABOUT YOUR APPEARANCE ENTIRELY.

PREPARE THE FOOD AS FAR IN ADVANCE AS POSSIBLE.

COFFEE CAN ALSO BE MADE SEVERAL HOURS BEFORE IT IS NEEDED, PROVIDED THE MILK IS NOT ADDED TO IT. BE SURE TO MAKE PLENTY!

AS WELL AS THE USUAL SANDWICHES, MAKE SOME OF THE OPEN DANISH VARIETY. USE WELL-BUTTERED, THICKISH SLICES OF WHOLEMEAL BREAD AND HEAP THEM UP WITH HAM, CHEESE, SARDINES AND SO ON. THESE ARE BEST EATEN WITH A KNIFE AND FORK.

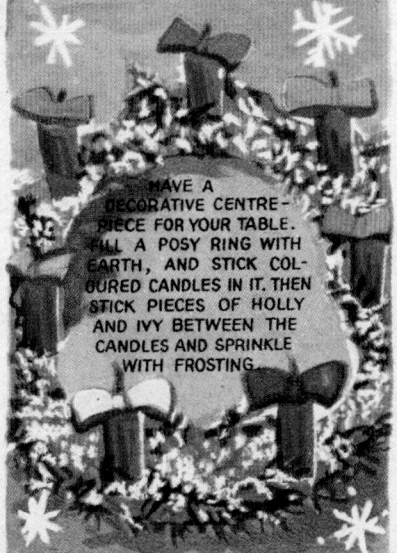

HAVE A DECORATIVE CENTRE-PIECE FOR YOUR TABLE. FILL A POSY RING WITH EARTH, AND STICK COLOURED CANDLES IN IT. THEN STICK PIECES OF HOLLY AND IVY BETWEEN THE CANDLES AND SPRINKLE WITH FROSTING.

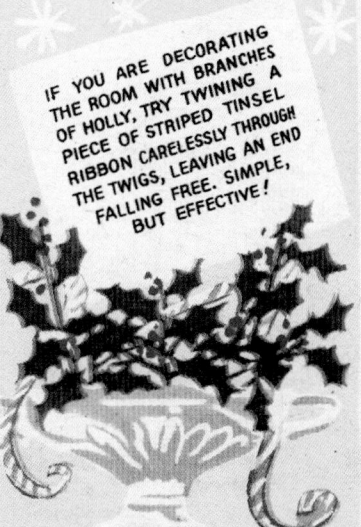

IF YOU ARE DECORATING THE ROOM WITH BRANCHES OF HOLLY, TRY TWINING A PIECE OF STRIPED TINSEL RIBBON CARELESSLY THROUGH THE TWIGS, LEAVING AN END FALLING FREE. SIMPLE, BUT EFFECTIVE!

WHEN YOUR PARTY STARTS, DO KEEP AN EYE ON THE SHY PEOPLE AND SEE THAT THEY ARE DRAWN INTO THINGS. IF YOU MENTION GUESTS' SPECIAL HOBBIES OR INTERESTS WHEN INTRODUCING THEM, IT GIVES A STARTING POINT FOR CONVERSATION.

Concerning YOU

THE COMMON COLD

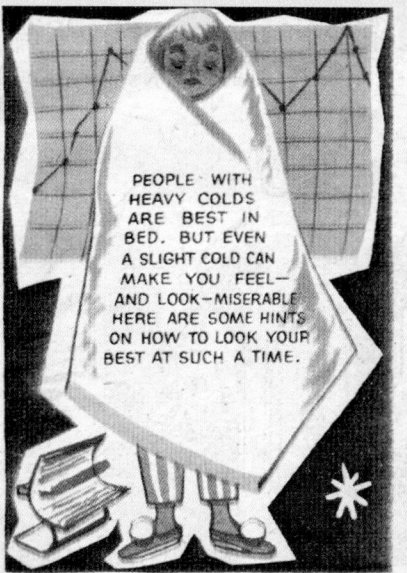

PEOPLE WITH HEAVY COLDS ARE BEST IN BED. BUT EVEN A SLIGHT COLD CAN MAKE YOU FEEL— AND LOOK—MISERABLE HERE ARE SOME HINTS ON HOW TO LOOK YOUR BEST AT SUCH A TIME.

USE ONLY PAPER HANDKERCHIEFS, THE TRIPLE-TEXTURED ONES SPECIALLY MADE FOR THE JOB. YOUR NOSE WON'T LOOK SO MUCH LIKE A CARROT IF YOU BLOW IT ON A DRY TISSUE INSTEAD OF A SOGGY, GERM-FILLED HANDKERCHIEF.

BORROW SOME OF MOTHER'S BARRIER CREAM (THE KIND FOR WET WORK) AND, FIRST THING IN THE MORNING, APPLY TWO COATS AROUND YOUR NOSE AND ALONG THE TOP LIP. NO MORE SORE NOSES!

AT BEDTIME, MASSAGE CAMPHOR ICE INTO THE SKIN ROUND THE NOSTRILS AND OVER THE BRIDGE OF THE NOSE. THIS WILL SOOTHE ANY REDNESS OR SORENESS AND MAY HELP TO RELIEVE CONGESTION.

HAIR-WASHING IS NOT ADVISABLE AT SUCH A TIME, SO GET RID OF THE 'BIRD'S NEST' LOOK BY DRY-CLEANING YOUR SCALP WITH A PAD OF COTTON WOOL, MOISTENED WITH COLOGNE. FOLLOW WITH A BRISK BRUSHING AND, IF YOU CURL YOUR HAIR, SET IN PIN CURLS IMMEDIATELY.

IF CONSTANT MOPPING AND BLOWING GIVES YOUR SKIN A BLOTCHY LOOK, ASK MOTHER FOR SOME OF HER TINTED FOUNDATION CREAM. APPLY IT IN TINY DOTS ALL OVER YOUR FACE AND STROKE IT IN THOROUGHLY.

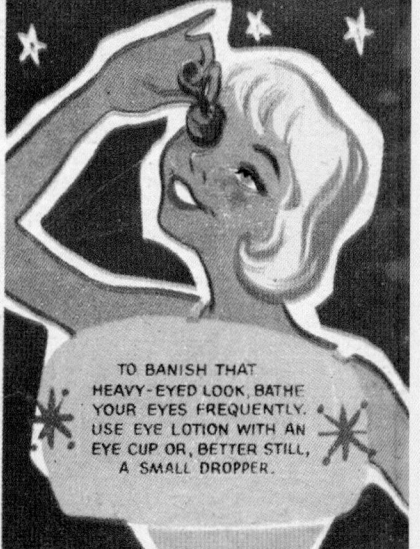

TO BANISH THAT HEAVY-EYED LOOK, BATHE YOUR EYES FREQUENTLY. USE EYE LOTION WITH AN EYE CUP OR, BETTER STILL, A SMALL DROPPER.

Concerning YOU

Care of your clothes

THE SECRET OF BEING WELL-DRESSED IS NOT TO HAVE MANY DRESSES, BUT TO LOOK AFTER THEM SO THAT THEY ARE ALWAYS FIT FOR WEARING. YOU CAN HAVE A WARDROBEFUL, BUT THEY WILL BE NO USE IF THERE IS SOMETHING WRONG WITH ALL OF THEM.

IT PAYS TO GROOM YOUR CLOTHES BEFORE YOU PUT THEM AWAY. BRUSH YOUR DRESS INSIDE AND OUT, WITH SPECIAL ATTENTION TO COLLAR AND CUFFS.

IT IS A TIME-SAVING IDEA TO KEEP A BOTTLE OF CLEANING STUFF IN YOUR BED-ROOM, AND GET RID OF ANY SPOTS ON CLOTHES AS SOON AS YOU TAKE THEM OFF.

PUT YOUR CLOTHES ON HANGERS, WHICH FIT THE SHOULDERS PROPERLY. FASTEN BUTTONS, ZIPPERS, SMOOTH DOWN COLLARS AND CUFFS. NOW AIR THEM OUTSIDE YOUR WARDROBE BEFORE YOU PUT THEM AWAY.

JERSEYS AND CARDIGANS NEED CARE TOO. THEY SHOULD NEVER BE HUNG UP, BECAUSE THEY ARE APT TO STRETCH AND LOOSE THEIR SHAPE. LIE THEM FLAT AND FOLD BACK THE SIDES AND SLEEVES.

IT IS BEST TO KEEP ALL JERSEYS IN PLASTIC CONTAINERS, OR WRAP THEM IN TISSUE PAPER, THEN LIE THEM FLAT IN A DRAWER. THEY WILL KEEP LOOKING FRESH AND NEW FOR MUCH LONGER.

Concerning YOU

ACCESSORIES

THE EFFECT OF THE PRETTIEST FROCK CAN BE RUINED IF YOU DON'T THINK OF THOSE EXTRAS CALLED "ACCESSORIES"— HATS, GLOVES, BELTS, HANDBAGS.

LET'S START FROM THE TOP. THE HAT THAT YOU TREASURE CAN BE KEPT IN SHAPE BY STUFFING THE CROWN WITH TISSUE PAPER BEFORE PUTTING IT AWAY IN YOUR WARDROBE.

A PRETTY BELT CAN LIVEN UP THE PLAINEST DRESS. SOMETIMES IT OUT-LIVES THE FROCK ITSELF AND CAN BE USED FOR A NEW ONE. BRUSH SUEDE BELTS WITH A SOFT BRUSH BEFORE PUTTING THEM AWAY. IT IS HANDY TO HAVE A SEPARATE COAT HANGER FOR BELTS ONLY.

WHITE GLOVES ALWAYS LOOK RIGHT—BUT THEY MUST BE GLEAMING WHITE! REMEMBER TO PULL THE FINGERS INTO SHAPE WHEN YOU TAKE THEM OFF.

HAVE A LOOK AT YOUR HANDBAG AND SEE WHAT A CURIOUS TREASURE HOUSE IT CAN BE! THAT IS, UNLESS YOU ARE FIRM WITH YOURSELF AND EMPTY YOUR BAG ONCE A WEEK.

GROOMING OF YOUR POSSESSIONS MAY SOUND A BORE, BUT IT WILL SAVE A LOT OF TIME IN THE END. SPEND TEN MINUTES IN PUTTING YOUR THINGS AWAY NEATLY WHEN YOU COME HOME AND NEXT TIME YOU GO OUT YOU WILL BE ABLE TO GET READY IN A PLEASANT, LEISURELY FASHION.

Concerning YOU

KEEPING WARM

FOR THE NEXT TWO MONTHS, THE WEATHER IS LIKELY TO BE COLD— BUT THERE'S NO NEED FOR YOU TO BE. ALWAYS REMEMBER THAT TWO THIN LAYERS OF CLOTHING ARE WARMER THAN ONE THICK ONE.

IT'S VERY IMPORTANT TO KEEP YOUR HANDS AND FEET WARM. WEAR A PAIR OF ANKLE SOCKS OVER YOUR STOCKINGS, AND, OUT OF DOORS, TWO PAIRS OF GLOVES—A THIN COTTON PAIR WITH A WOOLY PAIR OVER THEM.

DRESSING FOR PARTIES IN COLD WEATHER CAN BE A PROBLEM. HOW-EVER, THERE ARE MANY LIGHT WOOL DRESSES ON THE MARKET, AND FOR OLDER GIRLS NOTHING LOOKS BETTER THAN A FELT SKIRT AND A SWEATER.

DON'T FORGET TO EAT PLENTY OF MILK, FISH, MEAT AND EGGS AS WELL AS STARCHY THINGS LIKE POT-ATOES. IF YOU'RE PRONE TO COLDS, TAKE HALIBUT LIVER OIL CAPSULES.

GET YOUR CIRCULATION REALLY WORKING EARLY IN THE DAY. DO EXERCISES WHEN YOU GET UP. WALK BRISKLY, OR EVEN RUN PART OF THE WAY TO SCHOOL OR WORK. YOU'LL FEEL FINE AFTERWARDS.

THE COLD MAY MAKE YOUR LIPS CRACK. GUARD AGAINST THIS BY RUBBING THEM WITH COLD CREAM OR COLOURLESS LIP SALVE BEFORE YOU GO OUT. IF YOU WEAR MAKE UP, USE A GREASY LIPSTICK AND RUB IN COLD CREAM AT NIGHT.

FINALLY, WHEN YOU ARE OUT IN THE COLD, HOLD YOURSELF WELL AND BREATHE DEEPLY — YOU'LL FIND YOU ACTUALLY ENJOY IT!

Concerning YOU

Hair Styles

HAVING DEALT WITH ROUTINE HAIR CARE LAST WEEK, HERE ARE A FEW SUGGESTIONS ABOUT STYLING YOUR HAIR TO SUIT YOUR FEATURES.

GIRLS WITH ROUND FACES SHOULD AVOID FUSSY CURLS AT THE SIDES, AS THESE ADD TO THE DUMPLING EFFECT. BRUSH THE SIDES SMOOTHLY, UPWARDS AND BACK, AND TRY A WISPY FRINGE IF YOUR FOREHEAD IS NOT TOO LOW.

IF YOU HAVE A ROUND FACE WITH LONG PLAITS YOU MIGHT LIKE THIS FOR A PARTY HAIR STYLE. DRAW THE PLAITS UP AND WIND INTO A CORONET ON TOP OF YOUR HEAD, PINNING SECURELY. A SHORT CURLY FRINGE IS ESSENTIAL. OTHERWISE IT WOULD BE TOO SEVERE.

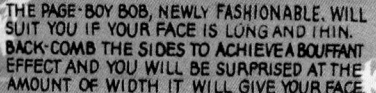

THE PAGE-BOY BOB, NEWLY FASHIONABLE, WILL SUIT YOU IF YOUR FACE IS LONG AND THIN. BACK-COMB THE SIDES TO ACHIEVE A BOUFFANT EFFECT AND YOU WILL BE SURPRISED AT THE AMOUNT OF WIDTH IT WILL GIVE YOUR FACE.

LUCKY PEOPLE WITH HEART-SHAPED OR OVAL FACES CAN WEAR ALMOST ANY HAIR STYLE. BEAR IN MIND THAT SHORT STYLES ARE EASIER TO KEEP IN ORDER AND THAT A CENTRE PARTING WILL FLATTER SYMMETRICAL FEATURES.

IF YOUR FACE TENDS TO BE SQUARE, DON'T WEAR YOUR HAIR LONGER THAN EAR-LEVEL AND BRUSH THE CURLS UP. THE PARTING SHOULD BE ON THE SIDE OR DIAGONALLY ACROSS THE CROWN.

IF YOUR NOSE IS TOO LONG FOR YOUR LIKING, A FRINGE WHICH CURLS FORWARD WILL MAKE IT APPEAR SHORTER. NEVER WEAR A CENTRE PARTING IF YOU HAVE A DETERMINED SQUARE JAW. REMEMBER THAT THE TERM 'CASUAL' APPLIED TO HAIR STYLES DOES NOT MEAN 'SHAGGY'.

Concerning YOU

SUPPER PARTY By Candlelight

CALL YOUR NEXT PARTY A SUPPER PARTY BY CANDLELIGHT AND SEE HOW THRILLED ALL YOUR FRIENDS WILL BE. INSTEAD OF ASKING THEM TO TEA, ASK THEM TO COME FROM 6 O'CLOCK TO 9 O'CLOCK.

PUT SOME SMALL TABLES INTO THE ROOM WHERE YOU WILL EAT, AND LAY THEM WITH COLOURFUL CHECKED CLOTHS OR CHECKED PAPER. WRITE OUT A MENU FOR EACH GUEST ON A PIECE OF WHITE CARDBOARD AND DECORATE THEM WITH ANY FANCY PATTERNS YOU CAN THINK OF.

YOU CAN ALSO MAKE SOME SIGNS TO HANG ON THE DOORS OF THE VARIOUS ROOMS. THESE WILL HELP YOUR GUESTS TO FIND THEIR WAY ABOUT THE HOUSE AND HELP TO CREATE A REAL PARTY ATMOSPHERE.

FIND ANY EMPTY CIDER OR BEER BOTTLES (LEAVE THE LABELS ON, IT WILL MAKE THEM LOOK JOLLIER) AND PUT A LARGE COLOURED CANDLE IN EACH OF THEM. PUT ONE OF THESE BOTTLES IN THE CENTRE OF EACH TABLE AND LIGHT THE CANDLES BEFORE YOU TAKE YOUR GUESTS IN TO SUPPER.

THE EASIEST SUPPER FARE, WHICH YOU CAN PREPARE WITHOUT ANYBODY'S HELP, IS HOT DOGS AND PICKLES. FOR THE HOT DOGS YOU NEED SOME LONG ROLLS AND CHIPOLATA SAUSAGES. CUT INTO THE ROLLS LENGTHWAYS, WITHOUT CUTTING THEM COMPLETELY IN TWO, AND PUT THE HOT SAUSAGES INTO THEM. PUT THE PICKLES IN LITTLE DISHES AND HAVE ONE DISH ON EACH TABLE.

AS A DESSERT YOU CAN EITHER HAVE FRUIT SALAD, OR A BIRTHDAY CAKE, IF THE PARTY IS FOR YOUR BIRTHDAY. GINGER POP IN TALL GLASSES WOULD BE A FITTING DRINK TO HAVE WITH YOUR SUPPER. BEFORE THE PARTY BREAKS UP, YOU COULD AUTOGRAPH EACH OTHERS MENU CARDS, SO THAT EVERYBODY CAN TAKE HOME A PLEASANT REMINDER OF THEIR FIRST SUPPER PARTY.

Concerning YOU

Clothes for the plump girl

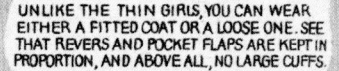

UNLIKE THE THIN GIRLS, YOU CAN WEAR EITHER A FITTED COAT OR A LOOSE ONE. SEE THAT REVERS AND POCKET FLAPS ARE KEPT IN PROPORTION, AND ABOVE ALL, NO LARGE CUFFS.

AVOID VIVIDLY CONTRASTING 'SEPARATES'. KEEP THE DARKER COLOUR FOR WHICHEVER PART OF YOU IS LARGEST. FOR EXAMPLE, IF YOU ARE TOP-HEAVY, CHOOSE, SAY, A BOTTLE GREEN SWEATER AND A MEDIUM GREY SKIRT.

WHEN SHOPPING FOR SUMMER DRESSES KEEP AWAY FROM HORIZONTAL STRIPES AND LARGE FLORAL PATTERNS. NARROW VERTICAL STRIPES ARE GOOD, SO ARE SPOTS AND SMALL ALL-OVER DESIGNS.

FRILLY CLOTHES AND TOO-FULL SKIRTS ARE NOT FLATTERING. BUT THE PRINCESS LINE (A FITTED DRESS WITH NO JOIN AT THE WAIST) WILL GIVE YOU SLIMNESS AND HEIGHT.

DON'T CHOOSE SATIN OR TULLE FOR A PARTY DRESS. THE FIRST IS ENLARGING, THE SECOND TOO FRAGILE. VELVETEEN IS BECOMING, SO IS LACE IF IT HAS A LINING TO MATCH.

PLEASE, NO PUFF SLEEVES PEASANT BLOUSES OR DRAINPIPE PANTS! GO FOR ONE-COLOUR DRESSES, SIMPLY CUT, AND YOU ARE BOUND TO LOOK SLIMMER.

Concerning YOU

Clothes for the TOO THIN GIRL

SEPARATES CAN BE A GOOD CAMOUFLAGE FOR THIN GIRLS. LOOK FOR HEAVY KNIT SWEATERS IN BRIGHT COLOURS. THOSE WITH TURTLE NECKS OR WRAP-OVER COLLARS ARE VERY GOOD.

PLEATED SKIRTS ARE FLATTERING IF YOUR HIPS ARE THIN. SUNRAY PLEATS SPRINGING FROM THE WAISTLINE WILL GIVE AN ILLUSION OF WIDTH.

AVOID FITTING COATS, PRETTY THOUGH THEY ARE. LOOK FOR ONE THAT FALLS STRAIGHT FROM THE SHOULDERS. I SUGGEST A DOUBLE-BREASTED STYLE WITH BIG POCKETS.

DON'T CHOOSE A FRILLY PARTY DRESS IN AN EFFORT TO DISGUISE THIN ARMS AND LEGS.

A FLUFFY ANGORA BOLERO OVER A SIMPLE DRESS IS MORE EFFECTIVE AND MUCH COSIER.

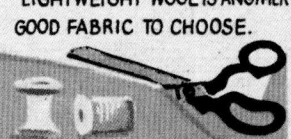

SOFT BULKY MATERIALS, SUCH AS CORDUROY, ARE BECOMING AND MAKE UP WELL INTO FULL-SKIRTED STYLES. PRINTED LIGHTWEIGHT WOOL IS ANOTHER GOOD FABRIC TO CHOOSE.

FOR A SMART PARTY OUTFIT, MAKE YOURSELF A CIRCULAR SKIRT IN VELVETEEN AND WEAR IT OVER A STIFF PETTICOAT. WEAR A SILK SHIRT BLOUSE WITH IT, AND PIN A RED OR PINK ROSE AT THE COLLAR.

Concerning YOU

Walking Holiday

THE HOLIDAY SEASON IS STARTING AGAIN NOW, AND HERE ARE SOME SUGGESTIONS FOR GIRLS GOING ON A WALKING TRIP.

THE MOST IMPORTANT ITEM IS FOOTGEAR. TAKE COMFORTABLE, STOUT, WALKING SHOES OR, BETTER STILL, BOOTS. IF YOU PLAN TO DO ANY CLIMBING, BOOTS ARE ESSENTIAL. TRY THEM ON WEARING THREE PAIRS OF SOCKS, ONE THIN AND TWO THICK, AND YOU CAN BE SURE OF TROUBLE-FREE FEET.

A PLEATED OR DIVIDED SKIRT IS COMFORTABLE TO WALK IN, AND SO ARE DENIM JEANS. SHORTS ARE NOT A GOOD IDEA AS THEY OFFER NO PROTECTION FROM A HOT SUN, OR FROM ROUGH COUNTRY AND UNDERGROWTH.

TAKE TWO OR THREE LONG-SLEEVED SHIRTS. THEY CAN BE ROLLED UP OR FASTENED AT THE WRIST IF THE SUN IS TOO HOT. A THICK SWEATER, A LIGHT-WEIGHT WATERPROOF, AND A HEADSCARF ARE ALL NECESSARY.

FOR EVENINGS, WHEN YOU MAY BE MEETING FRIENDS OR DANCING, TAKE A PLAIN DARK SWEATER AND TWO BRIGHT CIRCULAR SKIRTS. SANDALS COMPLETE THE OUTFIT.

cotton wool

EVEN THIS EARLY IN THE YEAR, PACK AN ANTI-SUN-BURN CREAM. IT IS A GOOD IDEA TO TAKE A JAR OF ALL-PURPOSE CREAM AS WELL, AND USE IT FOR CLEANING YOUR FACE IN THE EVENING. SOAP AND WATER CAN BE HARD ON A SUN-BURNED SKIN!

DON'T FORGET TALCUM POWDER AND SURGICAL SPIRIT FOR FOOT CARE, AND ADHESIVE PLASTERS FOR THE ODD BLISTER. FINALLY, REMEMBER YOU WILL PROBABLY BE CARRYING EVERYTHING ON YOUR BACK, SO ONLY PACK ESSENTIALS!

Concerning YOU

EASTER BUNNY

HAVE YOU NOTICED HOW MUCH DIFFERENCE THE WRAPPINGS MAKE TO A GIFT? PRESENT A BEAUTIFULLY DONE UP PARCEL TO A FRIEND AND SHE'S PLEASED EVEN BEFORE SHE OPENS IT!

EASTER EGGS AND A HANKY MAKE A NICE PRESENT— HOW MUCH MORE FUN IT WILL BE, FOR BOTH OF YOU, IF YOU MAKE AN 'EASTER BUNNY' OUT OF THE HANKY, AND HIDE THE EGGS INSIDE!

YOU WILL NEED A FAIRLY LARGE HANKY, 1 SAFETY PIN, SOME STIFF PINK PAPER, COLOURED RIBBON AND TWO BLACK BUTTONS.

FIRST, FOLD THE HANKY INTO A TRIANGLE. GET HOLD OF THE ENDS TO FORM EARS AND THEN TRANSFER THEM TO YOUR LEFT HAND. TAKE UP FREE ENDS WITH RIGHT HAND.

NOW FOLD BACK FREE ENDS AND TIE A RIBBON AT THE NECK, WHERE YOU HELD THE HANKY WITH YOUR LEFT HAND. YOUR BUNNY IS TAKING SHAPE NOW, SO STUFF THE PRESENTS DOWN THE SIDES TO MAKE IT STAND UP ON ITS OWN.

PIN THE BUNNY TOGETHER AT THE BACK. TO STIFFEN HIS EARS PUT A STRIP OF PINK PAPER INSIDE THEM. FINISH HIS FACE WITH BUTTON EYES AND A TINY, PINK PAPER, NOSE.

YOU CAN ALSO USE THIS BUNNY TO DECORATE THE TABLE FOR AN EASTER TEA-PARTY. MAKE ONE FOR EACH GUEST FROM TABLE NAPKINS AND FILL THEM WITH SWEETS.

Concerning YOU

Staying with friends

THE FUN OF STAYING WITH FRIENDS STARTS WHEN YOU PACK YOUR CASE. IT IS A GOOD IDEA TO FIND OUT WHAT CLOTHES YOU WILL NEED. YOUR FRIEND WILL BE ABLE TO TELL YOU.

IT IS A WELCOME AND POLITE GESTURE TO TAKE A LITTLE PRESENT TO YOUR FRIEND'S MOTHER. A SMALL BOX OF CHOCOLATES IS A GOOD CHOICE WHEN VISITING PEOPLE IN THE COUNTRY, BUT CHOOSE FLOWERS OR FRUIT FOR TOWNSPEOPLE.

IF YOU STAY FOR A FEW DAYS, THERE MAY BE TIMES WHEN ALL THE FAMILY ARE BUSY WITH THEIR HOBBIES. YOU WILL BE ABLE TO SETTLE INTO THE FAMILY CIRLE MORE NATURALLY IF YOU TAKE YOUR OWN KNITTING, NEEDLEWORK OR BOOK, WITH YOU.

EACH FAMILY HAS ITS OWN ROUTINE WITH MEALS. ADJUST YOURSELF AND ACCEPT IT, EVEN IF IT IS ENTIRELY DIFFERENT FROM HOME ROUTINE. THESE DIFFERENCES ADD AN EXTRA INTEREST TO YOUR STAY — YOU CAN SEE HOW OTHER FAMILIES LIVE.

IF YOU WANT TO GET THE 'GOOD GUEST DIPLOMA', AND BE ASKED AGAIN, REMEMBER THESE TWO POINTS. FIRST, DON'T BE SHY AND SPEECHLESS WHEN YOU ENJOY SOMETHING. SAY HOW MUCH YOU LIKED IT.
SECONDLY, ALWAYS STATE YOUR PREFERENCES WHEN ASKED FOR THEM. NEVER SAY, "I DON'T MIND". IT IS MUCH EASIER FOR EVERYBODY IF YOU GIVE A DEFINITE ANSWER.

FINALLY, WRITE YOUR 'THANK-YOU' LETTER AS SOON AS YOU GET HOME, WHILE THE MEMORIES OF YOUR STAY ARE FRESH IN YOUR MIND. LEAVING IT FOR A FEW DAYS ONLY MEANS A BAD CONSCIENCE — AND A MORE DIFFICULT LETTER TO WRITE!

Concerning YOU

Choosing a basic wardrobe

A LOOSE COAT SUITS ALL FIGURES. CHOOSE A SINGLE-BREASTED STYLE WITH RAGLAN SLEEVES IF YOU ARE PLUMP, AND A DOUBLE-BREASTED ONE WITH SET-IN SLEEVES IF YOU ARE THIN.

A TWEED SUIT WITH A STRAIGHT, HIP-LENGTH JACKET IS MOST USEFUL. WEAR IT WITH A BLOUSE IN THE SPRING AND WITH A THICK SWEATER IN THE AUTUMN.

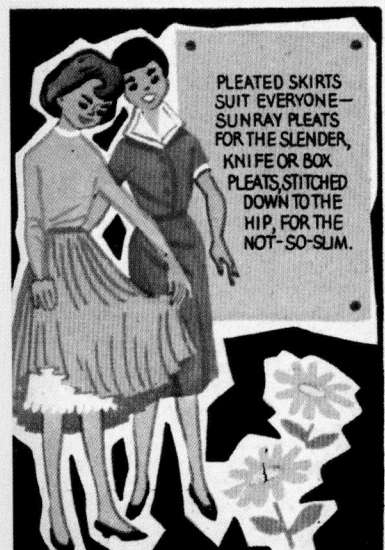

PLEATED SKIRTS SUIT EVERYONE — SUNRAY PLEATS FOR THE SLENDER, KNIFE OR BOX PLEATS, STITCHED DOWN TO THE HIP, FOR THE NOT-SO-SLIM.

BULKY SWEATERS ARE FASHIONABLE, AND ARE FUN TO MAKE. SEPARATES ARE THE EASIEST WAY OF EXPANDING YOUR BASIC WARDROBE.

YES

NO

THINK TWICE BEFORE BUYING BALLERINA SHOES — THEY CAN ENCOURAGE A WADDLE. BABY-HEELED COURT SHOES ARE ATTRACTIVE AND COMFORTABLE. THESE, AND A PAIR OF SENSIBLE LACE-UPS, WILL MEET ALL OCCASIONS.

PITFALLS TO AVOID ARE DUSTY BLACK SWEATERS, GRUBBY WHITE ACCESSORIES AND DIPPING HEMLINES.

AND AVOID DRAINPIPE SLACKS, UNLESS YOU ARE SLIM AND HAVE LONG LEGS.

Concerning YOU

Shampoo and Set

IF YOU CURL YOUR HAIR, HERE ARE SOME TIPS FOR YOUR WEEKLY SHAMPOO AND SET. YOU WILL NEED: SHAMPOO, TAIL-COMB, HAIR-BRUSH, PINS AND A HAIRNET. SPRING-CLIPS ARE USEFUL FOR HAIRS AT THE BACK OF THE NECK.

START BY WASHING YOUR BRUSH AND COMB. IT'S A WASTE OF TIME TO WASH YOUR HAIR AND THEN USE A GRUBBY BRUSH!

IF YOUR HAIR-BRUSH HAS PLASTIC BRISTLES, USE IT TO BRUSH THE SHAMPOO THROUGH YOUR HAIR. FINALLY RINSE AND RINSE!

PART YOUR HAIR AS USUAL AND PIN IT UP. TO MAKE A PIN-CURL, DIVIDE OFF A STRAND OF HAIR AND WIND IT UP INTO A 'SNAIL'. PIN IT FLAT WITH TWO HAIRPINS.

TO SET SHORT HAIR, MAKE TWO ROWS OF CURLS ALL ROUND, TURNING THE TOP ROW AWAY FROM THE FACE AND THE LOWER ONE TOWARDS IT. THIS GIVES A LASTING SET AND IS WELL WORTH PRACTISING. FINALLY COVER THE PINS WITH A HAIRNET.

FOR A CURLY FRINGE, COMB YOUR HAIR FORWARD AND DIVIDE IT INTO TWO LAYERS. SET THE UNDERNEATH LAYER TIGHTLY AND THE TOP ONE MORE LOOSELY. TURN BOTH ROWS TOWARDS THE PARTING. WHEN YOUR HAIR IS DRY, BRUSH IT HARD BEFORE COMBING IT INTO PLACE.

Concerning YOU

Make-up

* AT ABOUT FIFTEEN — WITH YOUR PARENTS' CONSENT — YOU CAN USE MAKE-UP FOR SPECIAL OCCASIONS. YOU WILL NEED: AN ALL-PURPOSE CREAM FOR DRY OR NORMAL SKINS, VANISHING CREAM FOR A GREASY ONE; POWDER IN A COLOUR WHICH TONES WITH YOUR SKIN, AND A LIGHT LIPSTICK.

WASH WITH MILD SOAP AND WARM WATER. RINSE WITH COLD AND PAT DRY. APPLY FOUNDATION CREAM IN TINY DOTS AND BLEND IN LIGHTLY. PRESS YOUR POWDER ON, AND REMOVE THE SURPLUS WITH CLEAN COTTON-WOOL.

TRY THIS FOR A SHINY NOSE. DISSOLVE A TEASPOONFUL OF SUGAR IN A TABLESPOONFUL OF BOILING WATER. LET IT COOL THEN STORE IT IN A BOTTLE. APPLY TO YOUR NOSE AND STROKE UNTIL IT FEELS SLIGHTLY STICKY. THEN POWDER.

wrong

right

ONLY PLUCK EYE-BROWS IF THEY MEET IN THE MIDDLE, AND THEN ONLY ENOUGH TO SEPARATE THEM. UNRULY BROWS CAN BE SMOOTHED DOWN WITH DAMP SOAP AND COMBED INTO PLACE. DARKEN VERY FAIR EYEBROWS WITH A BROWN PENCIL. USE SHORT, FEATHERY STROKES. NEVER A THIN, HARD LINE!

NOW FOR LIPSTICK OUTLINE THE TOP LIP CAREFULLY, FOLLOWING THE *NATURAL* CURVE. THEN SWEEP SMOOTHLY ACROSS THE LOWER LIP. PRESS THEM TOGETHER TO BLEND THE COLOUR, THEN BLOT WITH A PIECE OF TISSUE PAPER

NOW, CONFIDENT THAT YOU LOOK YOUR BEST, FORGET ABOUT YOUR MAKE-UP. CAREFULLY APPLIED, IT WILL LAST THE WHOLE EVENING. IF IT SHOULD NEED RETOUCHING, NEVER DO IT IN PUBLIC!

Concerning YOU

Colour Sense in Clothes

CHOOSING THE RIGHT COLOURS TO SUIT YOU CAN MAKE ALL THE DIFFERENCE TO YOUR APPEARANCE.

ALWAYS CONSIDER THE COLOUR OF YOUR HAIR AND EYES WHEN CHOOSING NEW CLOTHES. EXPERIMENT WITH VARIOUS COLOURS, DRAPING PIECES OF MATERIAL NEAR YOUR FACE TO FIND OUT WHICH SUITS YOU BEST.

NEVER FALL FOR A PRETTY COLOUR WITHOUT THINKING OF THE REST OF YOUR WARDROBE. WHAT IS THE USE OF A PRETTY BLOUSE IF YOU HAVE NO SKIRT TO WEAR WITH IT?

WRONG

IT IS A MISTAKE TO HAVE ALL YOUR ACCESSORIES IN ONE COLOUR.

RIGHT

BLENDING ACCESSORIES, WITH ONE SPLASH OF COLOUR, GIVE A MUCH SMARTER EFFECT.

COAT   SUIT

SKIRTS

SHO...

IT IS A HELP TO MAKE YOURSELF A 'COLOUR CHART' AND MARK YOUR BASIC WARDROBE ON IT. THIS WAY, YOU WILL MAKE FEWER MISTAKES WHEN SHOPPING.

ONE LAST PIECE OF ADVICE:—DO NOT COPY THE CLOTHES YOUR FRIENDS ARE WEARING.

BUY THINGS THAT WILL SUIT YOUR OWN COLOURING AND PERSONALITY.

Concerning YOU

Cycling Holiday

MAKE SURE THAT YOUR BICYCLE IS IN GOOD ORDER. GIVE IT A COMPLETE OVERHAUL A DAY OR TWO BEFORE SETTING OFF. FATHERS AND BROTHERS CAN HELP HERE!

PLAN YOUR ROUTE IN ADVANCE, AND DON'T TRY TO GO TOO FAR ON THE FIRST DAY. AVOID STIFFNESS BY DOING DAILY EXERCISES THE WEEK BEFORE YOUR HOLIDAY.

WEAR JEANS OR A DIVIDED SKIRT RATHER THAN SHORTS. THEY ARE JUST AS COMFORTABLE, AND PROTECT YOUR LEGS BETTER.

TAKE AT LEAST ONE HEAVY SWEATER, AND A WATERPROOF CAPE. A SOU'WESTER IS THE MOST EFFICIENT HEADGEAR FOR WET WEATHER.

LOOK AFTER YOUR EYES. TAKE SUN-GLASSES, OR AN EYESHADE, AND SOME EYE-LOTION IN A DROPPER-BOTTLE. USE IT AT THE END OF THE DAY.

SUNBURN CREAM IS ANOTHER ESSENTIAL—AND DO GIVE YOUR LEGS A GOOD HELPING. NOTHING IS MORE PAINFUL THAN BURNT KNEES!

Concerning YOU

Picnic

WEAR SUITABLE, COMFORTABLE CLOTHES. JEANS AND A SHIRT ARE IDEAL, BUT TAKE A HEAVY SWEATER IN CASE IT TURNS CHILLY.

SUNBURN CREAM AND AN INSECT REPELLENT WILL BE USEFUL, IF THE FORECAST SAYS 'RAIN' TUCK YOUR MAC INTO THE PICNIC BASKET

MAKE A CHANGE FROM THE USUAL SAND-WICHES. PACK A LONG FRENCH LOAF, BUTTER SEPARATELY WRAPPED, SOME SLICED SALAMI OR LIVER SAUSAGE, AND MAKE YOUR OWN SANDWICHES ON THE SPOT. FRENCH MUS-TARD, IN A TUBE, GOES WELL WITH THIS.

TO KEEP LETTUCE CRISP, PUT IT IN A POLYTHENE BAG AND FASTEN THE TOP. TAKE TWO VACUUM FLASKS — ONE OF ICED FRUIT JUICE AND ANOTHER OF HOT COFFEE.

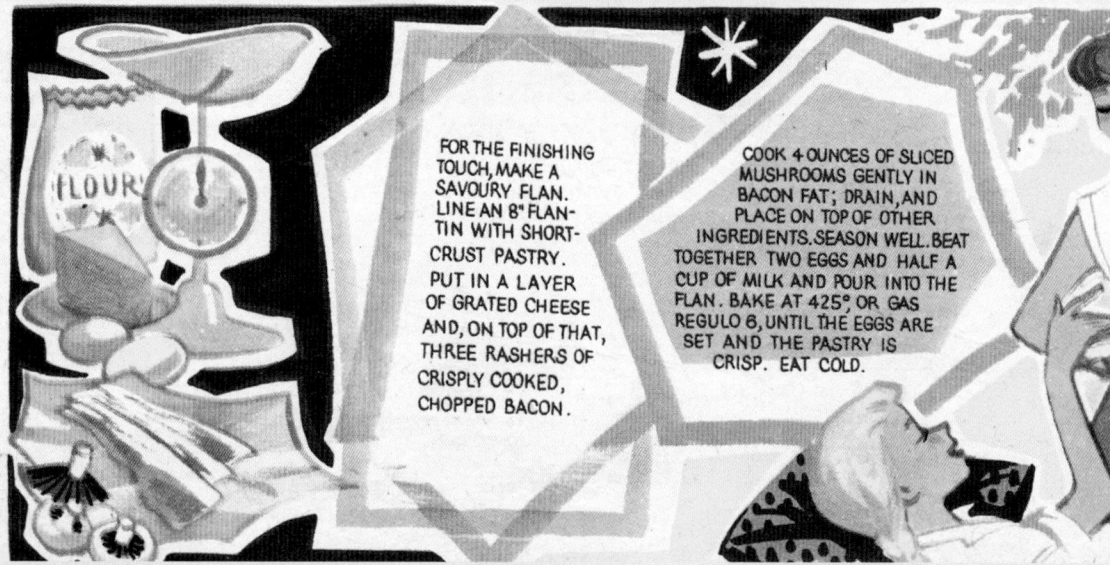

FOR THE FINISHING TOUCH, MAKE A SAVOURY FLAN. LINE AN 8" FLAN-TIN WITH SHORT-CRUST PASTRY. PUT IN A LAYER OF GRATED CHEESE AND, ON TOP OF THAT, THREE RASHERS OF CRISPLY COOKED, CHOPPED BACON.

COOK 4 OUNCES OF SLICED MUSHROOMS GENTLY IN BACON FAT; DRAIN, AND PLACE ON TOP OF OTHER INGREDIENTS. SEASON WELL. BEAT TOGETHER TWO EGGS AND HALF A CUP OF MILK AND POUR INTO THE FLAN. BAKE AT 425°, OR GAS REGULO 6, UNTIL THE EGGS ARE SET AND THE PASTRY IS CRISP. EAT COLD.

Concerning YOU

Sunbathing

WE ALL HOPE FOR A CHANCE TO LAZE IN THE SUN WHILE ON HOLIDAY. THERE ARE A FEW RULES TO BE FOLLOWED, HOWEVER, IF YOU ARE TO RETURN TANNED, AND NOT BURNT.

DON'T OVERDO YOUR SUNBATHING ON THE FIRST DAY. BETWEEN TEN AND TWENTY MINUTES' EXPOSURE IS ENOUGH TO BEGIN WITH. THEN LENGTHEN THE TIME GRADUALLY EACH DAY.

A SUN-FILTER CREAM IS NECESSARY FOR MOST TYPES OF SKIN. FAIR-SKINNED PEOPLE MUST USE IT GENEROUSLY. FOLLOW THE INSTRUCTIONS TO THE LETTER, AND IF THEY SAY 'REPEAT APPLICATION IN TWENTY MINUTES', THEN DO SO.

ALWAYS PROTECT YOUR HEAD. A SHAGGY STRAW HAT LOOKS ATTRACTIVE — SO DOES A COTTON SQUARE, FOLDED INTO A TRIANGLE, WITH THE ENDS KNOTTED BEHIND YOUR HEAD.

PROTECT YOUR EYES, TOO. BUY YOUR SUNGLASSES FROM AN OPTICIAN IF YOU CAN. HE WILL SEE THAT YOU GET THE RIGHT KIND. AN EYE-SHADE IS EVEN BETTER— THE KIND WORN BY TENNIS PLAYERS.

IF YOU HAVE A THIN, SENSITIVE SKIN WHICH TURNS BRIGHT RED IN THE SUN, BE SENSIBLE AND KEEP COVERED-UP. A PALE, COOL GIRL CAN LOOK MOST ATTRACTIVE IN A HEAT-WAVE.

Concerning YOU

Going Abroad

A LONG JOURNEY IS VERY TIRING, SO GO TO BED EARLY THE NIGHT BEFORE. TEN HOURS SLEEP SHOULD BE YOUR TARGET.

DON'T TRAVEL IN YOUR BEST CLOTHES. THE AMOUNT OF DUST AND CINDERS THAT COLLECT ON ONE'S PERSON IS FANTASTIC. AIM AT BEING NEAT, BUT COMFORTABLE.

ONCE THE CHANNEL IS CROSSED, ABANDON ALL THOUGHTS OF WASHING UNTIL THE JOURNEY IS OVER. PACK A SOAPY FACE-FLANNEL AND A MOIST SPONGE, AND USE THESE TO FRESHEN YOUR HANDS. TAKE CLEANSING PADS FOR FACE AND NECK AND, IF ANY WATER IS AVAILABLE, USE IT FOR CLEANING YOUR TEETH. FROZEN COLOGNE WILL KEEP YOU COOL.

REMEMBER THAT, IN HOT WEATHER, ANYTHING TIGHT WORN AROUND THE WAIST WILL BE VERY UNCOMFORTABLE. CHECK PANTIE ELASTIC AND SUSPENDER BELT, TOO.

IF YOU THINK IT'S IMPOSSIBLE TO FEEL COLD IN A HEAT WAVE, THEN YOU'VE NEVER SPENT A NIGHT IN A TRAIN. THE TEMPERATURE DROPS ALARMINGLY! PACK AN EXTRA-THICK SWEATER AND A PAIR OF SLIPPERS, IN THE TOP OF YOUR SUITCASE, AND DON THEM BEFORE SETTLING DOWN FOR THE NIGHT.

NO WHISTLE-BLAST SIGNALS THE DEPARTURE OF TRAINS ABROAD, THEY SIMPLY DRAW OUT ON TIME — SO MAKE SURE THAT YOU'RE IN YOUR SEAT EARLY. TAKE A FLASK OF COFFEE OR DILUTED FRUIT-JUICE WITH YOU. THESE THINGS BOUGHT ON STATIONS CAN RUN AWAY WITH YOUR FOREIGN CURRENCY.

Concerning YOU

THE GOOD GUEST

NEXT TIME YOU GO TO A PARTY, RESOLVE TO BE A GOOD GUEST — ONE TO WHOM THE HOSTESS CAN SAY SINCERELY, AFTER THE PARTY, 'THANK YOU FOR COMING'.

HAVE A WELCOMING SMILE ON YOUR FACE WHEN YOUR HOSTESS MAKES THE INTRODUCTIONS. TRY TO BE GENUINELY INTERESTED IN THE PEOPLE YOU MEET, AND YOU WILL BE SURPRISED HOW QUICKLY ALL SHYNESS AND STIFFNESS VANISHES.

IF IN DOUBT WHETHER TO USE A FORK OR A SPOON FOR A PUDDING, FOLLOW THE LEAD OF YOUR HOSTESS. BUT SHOULD YOU START WITH THE WRONG IMPLEMENT, JUST CARRY ON GAILY — NOBODY WILL MIND.

FIT YOURSELF INTO THE MOOD OF THE PARTY — EVEN IF YOU ARE NOT VERY INTERESTED IN THE ACTIVITIES YOUR HOSTESS HAS PLANNED. AFTER ALL, YOU CAN FOLLOW YOUR OWN INTERESTS AT HOME.

A PARTY IS NOT THE PLACE FOR WHISPERED CONVERSATIONS WITH YOUR BEST FRIEND. A LITTLE ISLAND OF TWO PEOPLE, WHO ARE ONLY INTERESTED IN ONE ANOTHER, CAN SPOIL ANY GATHERING.

WHEN IT IS TIME TO LEAVE, DON'T LINGER AWKWARDLY IN THE DOORWAY. YOU WILL ONLY BE A HINDRANCE TO YOUR HOSTESS. SAY YOUR THANKS AND GOODBYES — AND *GO!*

Concerning YOU

how to cope with depressions'

MANY OF YOU HAVE WRITTEN ASKING WHAT TO DO ABOUT CHANGES IN MOOD — ONE MINUTE FEELING UP IN THE AIR, THE NEXT MINUTE DOWN IN THE DEPTHS.

THE HAPPY MOODS ARE GREAT FUN, BUT DEPRESSIONS CAN BE UNPLEASANT. WHEN A DEPRESSION SETS IN, IT IS A GOOD PLAN TO TALK ABOUT IT WITH SOMEONE. GETTING IT OFF YOUR CHEST ALWAYS HELPS.

DON'T FORGET THAT DEPRESSION MAY HAVE A PHYSICAL CAUSE. MAKE SURE YOU ARE EATING THE RIGHT THINGS AND GETTING ENOUGH SLEEP. REMEMBER, TOO, THAT WHEN YOU ARE IN YOUR TEENS A LOT OF COMPLICATED CHEMICAL CHANGES ARE GOING ON IN YOUR BODY WHICH CAN CAUSE MOODINESS.

NEXT TIME YOU ARE DEPRESSED, TRY DOING SOMETHING DEFINITE, LIKE GOING FOR A WALK OR PLAYING TENNIS, OR WORKING AT A HOBBY.

IT IS A RARE DEPRESSION THAT CAN SURVIVE HARD EXERCISE OR CONCENTRATION.

FINALLY, DON'T WORRY ABOUT YOUR MOODS. THEY WON'T LAST FOR EVER! COMFORT YOURSELF WITH THE REFLECTION THAT EVERYONE IN THE WORLD HAS THIS PROBLEM AT SOME TIME OR ANOTHER.

Concerning YOU

HOW TO FOLLOW

THE FASHIONS

THE CHANGING WORLD OF FASHION FORMS PART OF THE GENERAL PICTURE OF AN ERA. IF YOU LOOK THROUGH THE PAPERS EACH SEASON YOU WILL SOON SEE THE TRENDS FASHION IS TAKING.

DO NOT THINK THAT IF YOU COULD AFFORD TO BUY AN ENTIRELY NEW SET OF CLOTHES EACH SEASON, YOU WOULD BECOME A WELL-DRESSED, ELEGANT GIRL. YOU WOULD LOOK OVER-DRESSED AND PERHAPS EVEN FUNNY.

A FASHION-CONSCIOUS GIRL'S FIRST RULE WILL BE SIMPLICITY. WAIT TILL A NEW FASHION IDEA 'CATCHES ON' BEFORE BUYING IT.

SOME FASHIONS LIVE ONLY FOR A MONTH AND LOOK SHOCKINGLY DATED THE THIRD TIME YOU WEAR YOUR NEW OUTFIT.

A GREAT AMOUNT OF SELF-DISCIPLINE IS NEEDED TO AVOID BUYING 'FATAL MISTAKES' BECAUSE THEY LOOKED ATTRACTIVE IN THE SHOP WINDOW.

IF YOU WANT TO LOOK OLDER AND MORE SOPHISTICATED WEAR COLOURFUL AND INTER-CHANGEABLE SEPARATES. DON'T TRY AND COPY OLDER WOMEN, AND WEAR SLEEK CLOTHES. YOU WILL LOOK JUST AS SILLY AS A MIDDLE-AGED WOMAN LOOKS IN TOO GIRLISH CLOTHES.

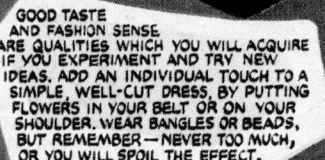

GOOD TASTE AND FASHION SENSE ARE QUALITIES WHICH YOU WILL ACQUIRE IF YOU EXPERIMENT AND TRY NEW IDEAS. ADD AN INDIVIDUAL TOUCH TO A SIMPLE, WELL-CUT DRESS, BY PUTTING FLOWERS IN YOUR BELT OR ON YOUR SHOULDER. WEAR BANGLES OR BEADS, BUT REMEMBER — NEVER TOO MUCH, OR YOU WILL SPOIL THE EFFECT.

MAKE SURE A NEW STYLE SUITS YOU, FROM *EVERY ANGLE*. NEVER GO IN FOR A NEW SHAPE UNTIL YOU SEE YOURSELF FROM THE BACK AND SIDES, TOO.

Concerning YOU

awkward figures

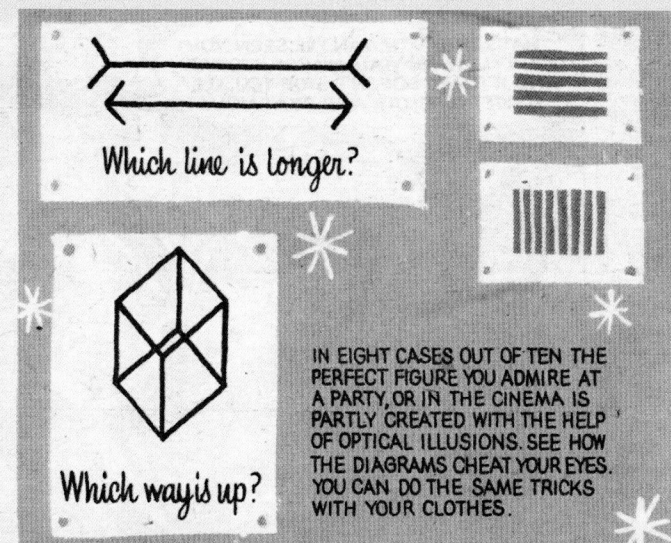

Which line is longer?

Which way is up?

IN EIGHT CASES OUT OF TEN THE PERFECT FIGURE YOU ADMIRE AT A PARTY, OR IN THE CINEMA IS PARTLY CREATED WITH THE HELP OF OPTICAL ILLUSIONS. SEE HOW THE DIAGRAMS CHEAT YOUR EYES. YOU CAN DO THE SAME TRICKS WITH YOUR CLOTHES.

YOU CAN SEE HOW THIS SAME IDEA WORKS IN NATURE. ANIMALS HIDE THEMSELVES BY BLENDING IN WITH THE COLOUR OF THEIR BACKGROUND. YOU CAN IMPROVE YOUR FIGURE IN EXACTLY THE SAME WAY.

NO

IF YOU ARE TOP HEAVY—THE MUSHROOM SHAPE—YOU HAVE TO PLAY DOWN YOUR BROAD SHOULDERS. DO NOT WEAR CLOTHES WHICH ARE FUSSY ABOVE THE WAIST AND, THEREFORE, DRAW ATTENTION TO YOUR WORST POINTS. HAVE ALL THE COLOUR AND FULLNESS IN YOUR SKIRT, AND KEEP YOUR TOP UNCLUTTERED AND SIMPLE. NEVER WEAR PADDED SHOULDERS OR PUFFED SLEEVES. TO MAKE UP FOR THE PLAINNESS OF YOUR BLOUSES YOU COULD WEAR UNUSUAL AND WIDE BELTS.

YES

NO

PERHAPS YOU HAVE NARROW SHOULDERS AND WIDE HIPS? THEN CONCENTRATE ON PRETTY NECKLINES AND WIDE COLLARS. FLARED OR STRAIGHT SKIRTS WILL SUIT YOU BETTER THAN BULKY ONES.

YES

FINALLY, ONCE YOU'VE CHOSEN A FLATTERING OUTFIT, FORGET YOUR FIGURE PROBLEMS. THEY'RE NOT NEARLY AS NOTICEABLE AS YOU THINK— AND HOW DULL IT WOULD BE IF WE ALL LOOKED ALIKE!

Concerning YOU

INTERVIEW FOR FIRST JOB

MANY OF YOU WILL HAVE LEFT SCHOOL THIS SUMMER, AND BE STARTING WORK. HERE ARE SOME POINTS TO REMEMBER WHEN APPLYING FOR A JOB. DRAFT A LETTER SETTING OUT YOUR QUALIFICATIONS AND ASKING FOR AN APPOINTMENT FOR AN INTERVIEW. THEN MAKE A COPY IN YOUR BEST HANDWRITING.

SITUATIONS VACANT

WHATEVER TIME OF THE YEAR IT IS, THERE ARE THREE THINGS YOU MUST WEAR —STOCKINGS, GLOVES AND A HAT.

IMPORTANT

DO NOT WEAR JANGLING JEWELLERY! YOU MIGHT BE GIVEN A TYPING TEST, AND WHAT WITH THE TYPEWRITER AND YOUR CHARM BRACELET, YOU WILL BE DUBBED A NOISY YOUNG WOMAN WITHOUT HAVING SAID A WORD!

A LITTLE MAKE-UP WILL HELP TO GIVE YOU CONFIDENCE, BUT DON'T OVERDO IT. EAU-DE-COLOGNE OR LAVENDER WATER ON YOUR HANDKERCHIEF IS ALSO GOOD FOR YOUR MORALE.

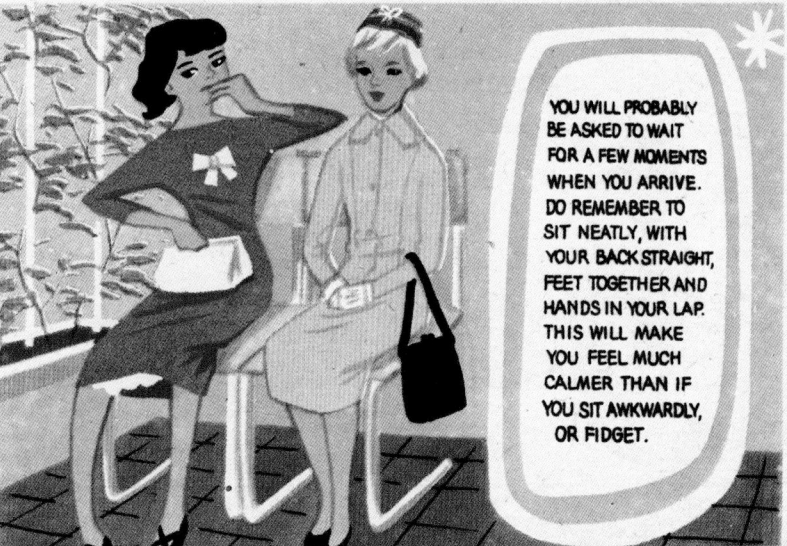

YOU WILL PROBABLY BE ASKED TO WAIT FOR A FEW MOMENTS WHEN YOU ARRIVE. DO REMEMBER TO SIT NEATLY, WITH YOUR BACK STRAIGHT, FEET TOGETHER AND HANDS IN YOUR LAP. THIS WILL MAKE YOU FEEL MUCH CALMER THAN IF YOU SIT AWKWARDLY, OR FIDGET.

MANAGER

ARRIVE PUNCTUALLY, THEN RELAX AND BE NATURAL DURING YOUR INTERVIEW. EITHER EXTREME SHYNESS OR OVERCONFIDENCE MAKE IT DIFFICULT FOR ANYONE TO JUDGE YOUR CAPABILITIES.

Concerning YOU

The Art of SOCIAL POISE

THAT ELUSIVE QUALITY CALLED 'POISE' OFTEN TAKES YEARS TO LEARN. BUT HERE ARE A FEW TRICKS WHICH WILL HELP YOU TO AVOID AWKWARD MOMENTS.

YOUR FIRST SAFEGUARD IS TO DRESS SUITABLY AND CAREFULLY. NOTHING MAKES ONE FEEL CLUMSIER THAN HAVING TO FIDGET WITH A COLLAR OR TRYING TO TUCK IN A BLOUSE.

PEOPLE TEND TO FIDGET WHEN THEY ARE NERVOUS. YOU CAN HELP YOURSELF RELAX BY SITTING DOWN GRACEFULLY AND COMFORTABLY. LET YOUR HANDS LIE TOGETHER, PALMS UPWARDS IN YOUR LAP.

SOME PEOPLE FIND IT DIFFICULT TO WALK ACROSS A ROOM WITHOUT KNOCKING INTO THINGS. IF THIS IS YOUR PROBLEM WHY NOT SET UP AN OBSTACLE COURSE AT HOME, AND PRACTISE ON IT?

ALWAYS CONCENTRATE ON THE PERSON WHO IS TALKING TO YOU. YOU WILL LOOK RESTLESS AND UNEASY IF YOU LET YOUR EYES ROAM AROUND THE ROOM. DON'T GO TO THE OPPOSITE EXTREME, HOWEVER, AND TRANSFIX THEM WITH A STEADY GLARE!

IF YOU HAVE TO PUT DOWN YOUR GLOVES AND OTHER BELONGINGS, DO PUT THEM SOMEWHERE ACCESSIBLE. IT SAVES TROUBLE FOR EVERYONE!

Concerning YOU

Making friends with boys

IT IS NATURAL TO WANT TO MAKE FRIENDS WITH BOYS, BUT GIRLS ARE SOMETIMES SHY ABOUT THIS — PARTICULARLY WHEN THERE ARE NO BOYS IN THEIR FAMILY.

IF YOU DO NOT KNOW ANY BOYS, AND ARE RATHER SHY ABOUT MEETING THEM, WHY NOT JOIN A MIXED YOUTH CLUB? THERE'S NOTHING LIKE SHARING INTERESTS AND ACTIVITIES TO BREAK DOWN SHYNESS.

TO GET TO KNOW A BOY BETTER, ARRANGE A SMALL PARTY AND ASK HIM TO IT ALONG WITH OTHER FRIENDS.

WHEN GETTING TO KNOW A BOY, ASK HIM ABOUT HIS INTERESTS AND *LISTEN* TO HIS ANSWERS. DON'T FEEL YOU HAVE TO DO ALL THE TALKING! THIS IS ONLY POLITE WITH FRIENDS OF EITHER SEX.

FINALLY, IF YOU FIND YOURSELF WITH A GROUP YOU DO NOT KNOW VERY WELL, JUST BE NATURAL. THE ICE WILL SOON BREAK. DON'T FORGET THAT BOYS ARE OFTEN SHY TOO!

Concerning YOU

SEWING CIRCLE

IF YOU WANT TO ENLARGE YOUR WARDROBE WITHOUT SPENDING TOO MUCH, WHY NOT FORM A SEWING CIRCLE WITH A FEW FRIENDS?

EVEN THE OLDEST SEWING MACHINE CAN SAVE HOURS OF LABOUR. MANY FAMILIES HAVE ONE TUCKED AWAY SOMEWHERE. ASK PERMISSION TO RESCUE IT AND HAVE IT OVERHAULED.

START A COMMON FUND TO BUY PAPER PATTERNS, PINS, ETC. STEEL DRESSMAKERS' PINS ARE ESSENTIAL, AND ALSO THREE SHADES OF TACKING THREAD.

IT IS A GOOD IDEA TO START WITH SOMETHING SIMPLE, SUCH AS A CIRCULAR SKIRT FOR PARTIES OR A DIRNDL FOR THE BEACH.

A PATTERN FOR A STRAIGHT SKIRT CAN ALSO SUPPLY YOU WITH A WAIST-SLIP.

TRY AND SAVE INDIVIDUALLY FOR THE JULY AND JANUARY SALES. THE BEST BARGAINS ARE NEARLY ALWAYS IN THE FABRICS DEPARTMENT.

IF YOU USE INGENUITY, YOU WILL NOT NEED MANY PATTERNS. MOST OF THEM CAN BE MADE UP IN AT LEAST TWO STYLES.

SALE

REDUCTION

REMNANTS

Concerning YOU

How to stand, walk and sit

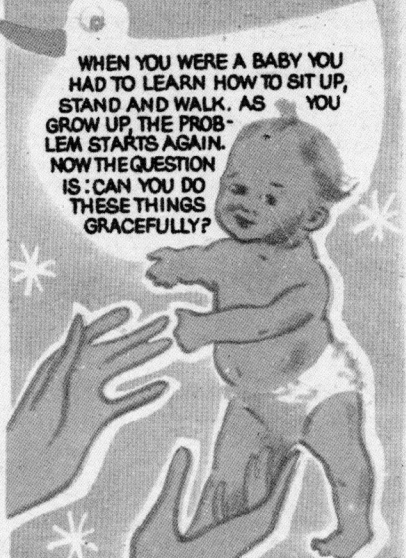

WHEN YOU WERE A BABY YOU HAD TO LEARN HOW TO SIT UP, STAND AND WALK. AS YOU GROW UP, THE PROBLEM STARTS AGAIN. NOW THE QUESTION IS: CAN YOU DO THESE THINGS GRACEFULLY?

KEEP YOUR POSTURE ERECT AS YOU SIT, AND YOUR SHOULDERS RELAXED. YOUR SPINE SHOULD BE SUPPORTED BY THE CHAIR BACK, YOUR TUMMY PULLED IN.

AS A GENERAL RULE, SIT WITH YOUR LEGS TOGETHER AND ONE FOOT JUST A LITTLE AHEAD OF THE OTHER. IF YOU CROSS YOUR LEGS, CROSS THEM HIGH ON THE THIGH SO THAT THEY ARE PARALLEL FROM THE KNEE DOWN.

A MODEL LEARNS DEPORTMENT, JUST AS GRANDMOTHER DID, BY WALKING WITH A BOOK ON HER HEAD. WHY NOT PRACTISE THIS IN YOUR ROOM?

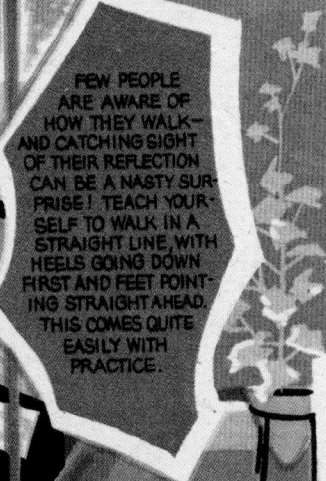

FEW PEOPLE ARE AWARE OF HOW THEY WALK— AND CATCHING SIGHT OF THEIR REFLECTION CAN BE A NASTY SURPRISE! TEACH YOURSELF TO WALK IN A STRAIGHT LINE, WITH HEELS GOING DOWN FIRST AND FEET POINTING STRAIGHT AHEAD. THIS COMES QUITE EASILY WITH PRACTICE.

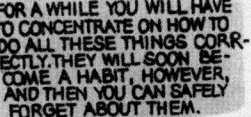

FOR A WHILE YOU WILL HAVE TO CONCENTRATE ON HOW TO DO ALL THESE THINGS CORRECTLY. THEY WILL SOON BECOME A HABIT, HOWEVER, AND THEN YOU CAN SAFELY FORGET ABOUT THEM.

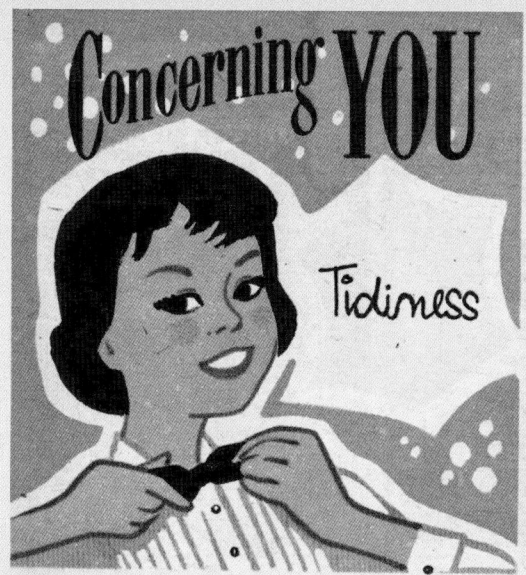

Concerning YOU

Tidiness

SOME PEOPLE FIND IT EASY TO BE TIDY—OTHERS DON'T! HERE ARE SOME TIPS FOR THOSE WHO FIND TIDINESS AND GOOD GROOMING FAR FROM SECOND NATURE.

SETTLE FOR A CASUAL LINE IN CLOTHES RATHER THAN A TAILORED ONE. KEEP ELEGANT OUTFITS FOR SPECIAL OCCASIONS.

YES

NO

YOU WILL FIND TWEED EASIER TO WEAR THAN PLAIN FABRICS. NAVY AND BLACK HAVE TO BE KEPT IMMACULATE, BUT FLECKED FABRICS AND GREYS DON'T SHOW THE DIRT.

IF YOUR STOCKING SEAMS INSIST ON SWERVING SIDEWAYS, GO IN FOR SEAMLESS ONES.

IF YOU LOOK AROUND, YOU WILL SEE MORE AND MORE SMART GIRLS WEARING THEM.

SHORT HAIR IS ALWAYS EASIER TO MANAGE THAN LONG HAIR.

IT'S WORTH SAVING TO HAVE IT CUT BY A REALLY GOOD HAIRDRESSER.

THESE THINGS WILL DISGUISE THE SLAPDASH LOOK—BUT GOOD GROOMING IS A HABIT—WHICH CAN BE ACQUIRED. SET YOURSELF A TARGET—LIKE KEEPING YOUR HANDS BEAUTIFULLY MANICURED EVERY DAY FOR A MONTH.

JUNE

SOON YOU WILL FIND THAT YOU LOOK AFTER YOUR HANDS QUITE AUTOMATICALLY. THEN IT IS TIME TO START SOMETHING ELSE.

TAKE THINGS SLOWLY HOWEVER, AND DON'T BE DISCOURAGED IF YOU BACKSLIDE OCCASIONALLY.

Concerning YOU

Ring the Changes with one Basic Dress

ONE PLAIN, V-NECKED DRESS CAN DO THE SERVICE OF SEVERAL SMART FROCKS FOR THE GIRL WITH FASHION SENSE.

FOR COLD DAYS, WEAR IT WITH A JERSEY POLO-NECK INSET, IN A CONTRASTING COLOUR.

FOR A DRESSIER EFFECT WEAR YOUR NICEST WHITE BLOUSE UNDER THE DRESS AND PUT A SMALL, BLACK VELVET RIBBON BOW ON THE COLLAR.

YOU CAN GO ONE STEP FURTHER AND BUY SPECIAL DETACHABLE COLLAR AND CUFFS TO MAKE YET ANOTHER TRANSFORMATION.

THE DRESS, WORN WITH A TWEED BOX-JACKET, CAN RE-PLACE A SUIT. A SCARF IN THE NECK WILL COM-PLETE THE OUTFIT.

TO TRANSFORM YOUR BASIC DRESS FOR A PARTY, DRAPE WHITE ORGAN-ZA, TULLE OR VELVET WIDELY ROUND THE NECKLINE. TIE A BIG BOW IN FRONT. LEAVE THE ENDS FLOATING.

Concerning YOU

Care of Spectacles

YOU SHOULD LEARN HOW TO HOLD SPECTACLES WHEN CLEANING THEM. GRASP THE FRAME AT THE TOP AND BOTTOM OF THE LENS, AS ILLUSTRATED. NEVER HOLD THEM BY THE BRIDGE. THIS IS THE COMMONEST CAUSE OF BREAKAGES.

ALWAYS USE BOTH HANDS FOR TAKING YOUR GLASSES OFF. OTHERWISE, THEY TEND TO GET OUT OF ALIGNMENT ONE SIDE AND EVENTUALLY BREAK AT THE SIDES.

IF YOU ONLY WEAR GLASSES FOR READING BE SURE TO PUT THEM STRAIGHT INTO A CASE WHEN YOU TAKE THEM OFF.

IF YOU SLIP THEM INTO A POCKET, SOONER OR LATER YOU WILL HAVE A BREAKAGE.

IF YOU HAVE A GREASY SKIN, TAKE EXTRA CARE OVER CLEANING YOUR SPECTACLES, AS THE GREASE GETS ON TO THEM AND ATTRACTS DIRT. THE PROFESSIONAL WAY TO DO IT IS TO WIPE THEM WITH COTTON-WOOL SOAKED IN METHYLATED SPIRITS, AND THEN POLISH WITH A SOFT CLOTH.

METH.

IF SOMETHING GOES WRONG, NO DO-IT-YOURSELF REPAIRS, PLEASE. A BENT PIN REPLACING A LOST SCREW, FOR INSTANCE, CAN CAUSE A THREAD TO STRIP AND MAKE THE FINAL REPAIR MUCH BIGGER.

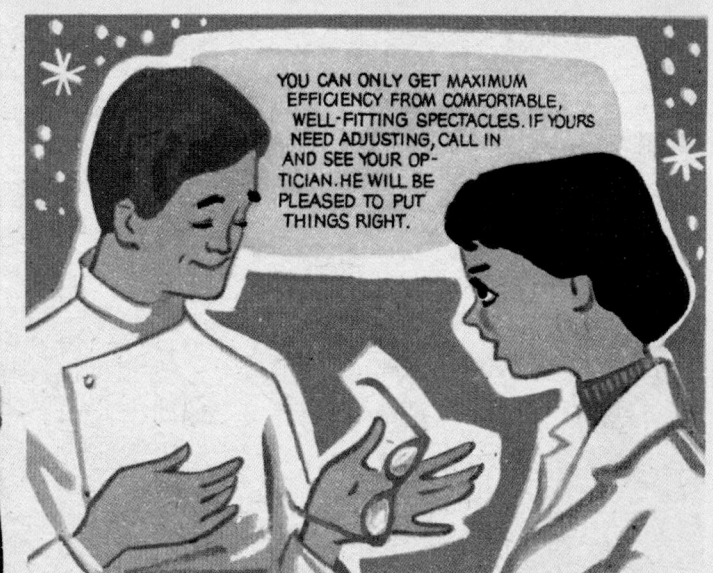

YOU CAN ONLY GET MAXIMUM EFFICIENCY FROM COMFORTABLE, WELL-FITTING SPECTACLES. IF YOURS NEED ADJUSTING, CALL IN AND SEE YOUR OPTICIAN. HE WILL BE PLEASED TO PUT THINGS RIGHT.

Concerning YOU

Smart Ways with Sweaters

ALWAYS WEAR LOOSE-FITTING SWEATERS AND JERSEYS. TIGHT ONES LOOK UNTIDY AND UNCOMFORTABLE.

YOU CAN 'DRESS-UP' THE PLAINEST JUMPER BY PINNING A GAY BROOCH ON IT.

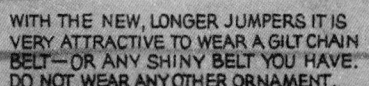

WITH THE NEW, LONGER JUMPERS IT IS VERY ATTRACTIVE TO WEAR A GILT CHAIN BELT—OR ANY SHINY BELT YOU HAVE. DO NOT WEAR ANY OTHER ORNAMENT.

A MATCHING BERET AND SCARF LOOK VERY SMART WITH A PLAIN SWEATER. STOP YOUR SCARF SLIPPING BY ANCHORING IT WITH TINY SAFETY PINS—BUT DON'T LET THEM SHOW!

FOR OLDER GIRLS, BEADS LOOK CHARMING, EVEN OVER A TAILORED JUMPER. WEAR THEM THE NEW WAY—ONE LONG ROW TIED IN A KNOT HALFWAY DOWN.

REMEMBER THAT TWINSETS LOOK MORE ORIGINAL IN CONTRASTING COLOURS—AND, UNLESS YOU FEEL VERY COLD, DO NOT BUTTON THE CARDIGAN ALL THE WAY.

Concerning YOU

Country Visit and Going to Church

Country Visit

LIFE IN THE COUNTRY IS A LITTLE MORE CONVENTIONAL THAN IN TOWNS, SO LEAVE YOUR JEANS AND DRAINPIPE PANTS AT HOME. A TWEED SKIRT WITH A TWINSET OR A THICK SWEATER IS IDEAL.

FOR WALKING, TAKE A PAIR OF LOW-HEELED, STOUT SHOES — AND THICK STOCKINGS OR KNEE-LENGTH SOCKS

TAKE A BERET OR HEADSCARF TO KEEP YOUR HAIR IN ORDER, AND A PAIR OF STRING GLOVES LINED WITH WOOL.

Going to Church

CLOTHES FOR CHURCH SHOULD ALWAYS BE SIMPLE AND NEAT. JEWELLERY LOOKS RATHER OUT OF PLACE, SO WEAR A FLOWER IN YOUR BUTTON-HOLE INSTEAD.

IT IS TRADITIONAL TO WEAR GLOVES AND A HAT, THOUGH IN SOME CHURCHES HATS ARE NO LONGER ESSENTIAL. ALWAYS WEAR STOCKINGS OR SOCKS.

MANY PEOPLE LIKE TO SAVE A NEW OUTFIT FOR A SPECIAL FESTIVAL BUT APART FROM THIS, CHURCH-GOING SHOULD NOT BE TURNED INTO A FASHION PARADE.

Concerning YOU

Clothes for Special Occasions

Visit to the Theatre

REMEMBER THAT YOU WILL BE SITTING DOWN FOR A LONG TIME, SO CHOOSE SOMETHING CREASE-RESISTING. DON'T WEAR A PARTY DRESS UNLESS YOUR COMPANIONS ARE IN EVENING DRESS.

THIS IS A GOOD OPPORTUNITY TO WEAR YOUR CHRISTMAS OR BIRTHDAY PRESENT JEWELLERY: A BROOCH, A NECKLACE OR BRACELET, PERHAPS—BUT NOT ALL THREE!

A HAT IS NOT NECESSARY, BUT IF YOU WEAR ONE, REMEMBER TO TAKE IT OFF BEFORE THE PERFORMANCE BEGINS—AND KEEP YOUR COMMENTS ABOUT THE PLAY TILL THE INTERVAL.

Dinner in a Restaurant

A NOT TOO TWEEDY SUIT, OR AN AFTERNOON DRESS ARE CORRECT FOR DINING IN A RESTAURANT. HOWEVER, FOR A BIG CELEBRATION, SUCH AS A TWENTY-FIRST BIRTHDAY PARTY, WEAR YOUR PRETTIEST PARTY FROCK.

YOU WILL LEAVE YOUR COAT IN THE CLOAKROOM, SO TAKE A SMALL HANDBAG TO HOLD YOUR HANDKERCHIEF AND OTHER ODDMENTS. FISHING IN ODD PLACES FOR A HANDKERCHIEF IS DEFINITELY NOT DONE!

TO DRESS UP YOUR APPEARANCE A LITTLE, WEAR A SMALL SPRAY OF FRESH FLOWERS. IF YOU TELL THE FLORIST WHAT THE OCCASION IS AND WHAT YOU ARE WEARING, SHE WILL HELP YOU CHOOSE SOMETHING SUITABLE.

REMEMBER THAT, IN A RESTAURANT, YOU ARE ON VIEW TO THE PUBLIC AS WELL AS TO YOUR FRIENDS—SO PUT INTO PRACTICE ALL YOU HAVE LEARNT ABOUT GOOD GROOMING FROM 'CONCERNING YOU'.

Concerning YOU

Flower Arrangement

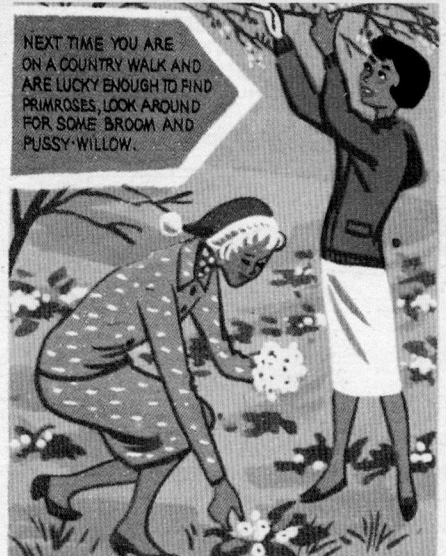

NEXT TIME YOU ARE ON A COUNTRY WALK AND ARE LUCKY ENOUGH TO FIND PRIMROSES, LOOK AROUND FOR SOME BROOM AND PUSSY-WILLOW.

CAREFULLY DIG UP A LITTLE CARPET OF MOSS AND PICK A FEW TRAILING STRANDS OF IVY.

WHEN YOU GET HOME, HUNT OUT AN OLD CHINA FIGURINE A CRINOLINE LADY OR A SHEPHERD WOULD BE IDEAL. WASH AND DRY IT CAREFULLY.

WITH YOUR WILD FLOWERS AND GREENERY, AND YOUR CHINA FIGURE, YOU CAN COMPOSE A VERY ATTRACTIVE FLOWER GROUP OR PICTURE.

USE AN OLD BREAD-BOARD AS A BASE. ARRANGE THE BROOM AND PUSSY-WILLOW AT THE BACK, IN A SMALL BOTTLE OF WATER. THEN PUT THE FIGURE IN POSITION. THE PRIMROSES, IN A TINY JAR, STAND IN FRONT.

COVER THE BOTTLES AND BASE WITH MOSS, THEN TRAIL A STRAND OR TWO OF IVY FROM EACH BOTTLE.

Concerning YOU

Natural Beautifiers

AN AGE-OLD SKIN-CLEANSER AND NOURISHER IS FRESH MILK. IF YOUR SKIN IS DRY AND SENSITIVE, SOAK A PAD OF COTTON-WOOL IN MILK AND WASH YOUR FACE WITH THIS, INSTEAD OF SOAP, BEFORE GOING TO BED. FINISH WITH A COLD WATER RINSE.

ONCE A WEEK, CLEAN YOUR TEETH WITH SALT. IT WILL TONE UP THE GUMS AND MAKE YOUR TEETH SPARKLING WHITE.

THE CUT HALF OF A LEMON RUBBED OVER YOUR HANDS IS SOFTENING AND WHITENING. IT ALSO WORKS WONDERS WITH ROUGH, RED ELBOWS.

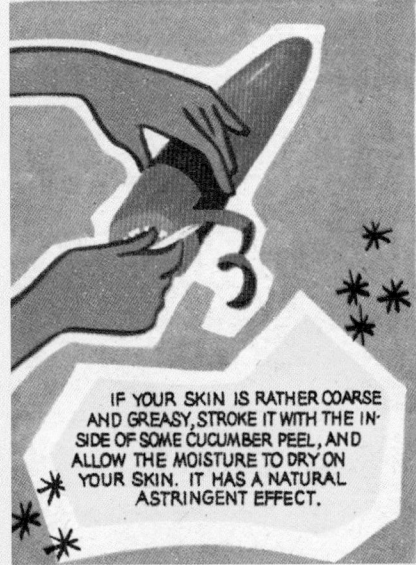

IF YOUR SKIN IS RATHER COARSE AND GREASY, STROKE IT WITH THE INSIDE OF SOME CUCUMBER PEEL, AND ALLOW THE MOISTURE TO DRY ON YOUR SKIN. IT HAS A NATURAL ASTRINGENT EFFECT.

FOR DULL, DRY HAIR TRY AN OCCASIONAL EGG SHAMPOO. WET THE HAIR WITH *LUKEWARM* WATER, AND RUB IN THE LIGHTLY-BEATEN YOLK (NO WHITE). LEAVE TO SOAK FOR A FEW MOMENTS, THEN RINSE THOROUGHLY WITH LUKEWARM WATER.

SOAK TIRED, ACHING FEET IN HOT WATER SOFTENED WITH SODA. THEN MASSAGE CASTOR OIL INTO THE SOLES. IT'S GOOD FOR BRITTLE TOENAILS, TOO.

BRUNETTES SHOULD END A SHAMPOO WITH A VINEGAR RINSE FOR EXTRA BRIGHTNESS. IT IS EVEN MORE EFFECTIVE IF YOU PUT A HANDFUL OF MINT LEAVES IN A MUSLIN BAG AND STEEP THIS IN THE LIQUID FIRST.

Concerning YOU

Springtime

NEARLY EVERYONE WANTS SOMETHING NEW FOR SPRING. HERE ARE SOME IDEAS WHICH WILL MAKE YOU FEEL GAY AND SPRING-LIKE, BUT WHICH DON'T COST MUCH.

A NEW COLOUR IS ALWAYS REFRESHING. TRY HOME-DYEING AN OLD JERSEY OR BLOUSE. REMEMBER TO FOLLOW THE DIRECTIONS ON THE PACKET EXACTLY.

CHEER UP AN OLD DRESS WITH AN ARTIFICIAL FLOWER AND FLOWING, NARROW RIBBONS.

BUY A WHITE, STIFF COLLAR TO WEAR WITH ANY ROUND-NECKED DRESS OR JERSEY. TIE IT WITH A DASHING BOW.

PEP UP YOUR OLD SUIT WITH A GAY JABOT. USE A LARGE LACE HANKY OR SILK SQUARE AND FASTEN IT, IN THE CENTRE, TO THE COLLAR OF YOUR SUIT.

INVEST IN GLEAMING WHITE SHORTIE GLOVES AND A WHITE BERET. THEY WILL MAKE YOU LOOK AND FEEL LIKE A SPRING MORNING.

Concerning YOU

Saving for a Rainy Day

REGULAR SAVING—NO MATTER HOW SMALL THE AMOUNT—IS A GOOD HABIT TO GET INTO. ANY OLD TIN BOX AND A LITTLE WILL-POWER ARE SUFFICIENT TO START YOU ON YOUR WAY.

IF YOU FIND IT A TEMPTATION TO SPEND THOSE PENNIES AND SIXPENCES, TRY PUTTING AWAY EVERY COIN THAT BEARS THE DATE OF THE YEAR YOU WERE BORN.

OR, ALTERNATIVELY, YOU COULD POP EVERY THREEPENNY-PIECE YOU RECEIVE INTO YOUR BOX. IF YOU'RE TEMPTED TO OPEN YOUR MONEY-BOX AND SPEND THE CONTENTS...

...GET A BANK-BOX FROM THE POST OFFICE AND OPEN A SAVINGS ACCOUNT. THEN, WHEN YOU TAKE THE BOX THERE TO BE OPENED, THE MONEY WILL GO STRAIGHT INTO YOUR ACCOUNT.

PERHAPS YOUR POCKET-MONEY DOESN'T LEAVE ANY MARGIN AT ALL FOR SAVING. IN THAT CASE—EARN SOME!

LET NEIGHBOURS WITH YOUNG CHILDREN KNOW THAT YOU ARE AVAILABLE FOR BABY-SITTING.

CAR-CLEANING, TAKING A DOG FOR REGULAR WALKS, MOWING LAWNS, FRUIT PICKING AND BATHING A NEIGHBOUR'S DOG—ALL CHORES WHICH YOU COULD TAKE OVER, AND WHICH WOULD HELP TO SUPPLEMENT YOUR INCOME.

Concerning **YOU**

Towelling

Beach Bag

TO MAKE THE BAG, YOU WILL NEED: TWO STRIPS OF TOWELLING 34" LONG BY 7" WIDE, AND ONE 29" BY 7" AND TWO MORE STRIPS OF THE SAME MEASUREMENTS, IN ANY KIND OF COTTON MATERIAL, FOR LINING.

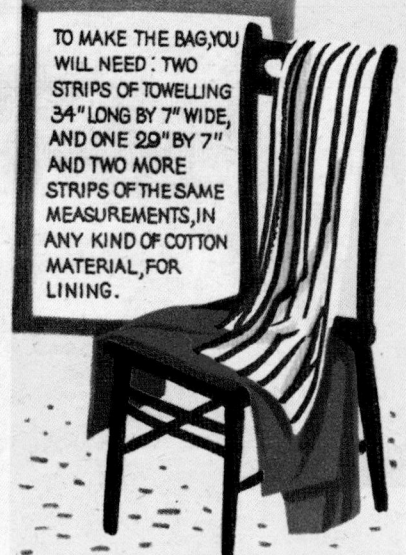

RIGHT SIDE OF LINING

RIGHT SIDE OF TOWELLING

LAY THE TOWELLING ON THE TABLE, RIGHT SIDE UP. PLACE THE LINING ON TOP, RIGHT SIDE DOWN. TACK TOGETHER AND THEN STITCH, LEAVING THE ENDS OPEN. YOU NOW HAVE TWO LONG TUBES.

TURN THEM INSIDE OUT AND PRESS. FOLD EACH ONE IN HALF, KEEPING THE LINING ON THE OUTSIDE.

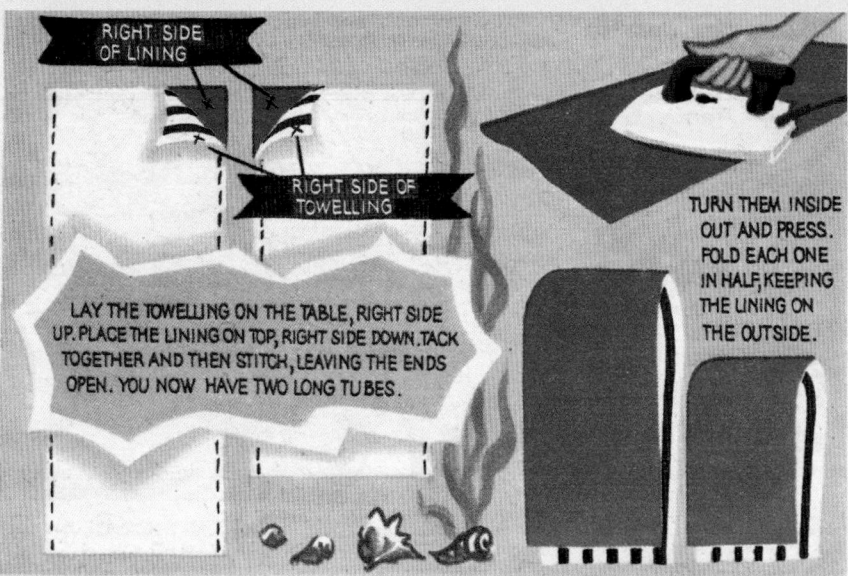

PLACE THEM SIDE BY SIDE, WITH THE CUT EDGES LEVEL. NOW STITCH CENTRE EDGES TOGETHER TO A DEPTH OF TEN INCHES TO FORM CENTRE SEAM BACK AND FRONT.

10"

10

9½"

STITCH OUTER EDGES TOGETHER TO A DEPTH OF 10" ON THE LONG SIDE AND 9½" ON THE SHORT SIDE TO FORM THE SIDE SEAMS. STITCH FIRMLY ALONG THE CUT EDGES TO MAKE THE BOTTOM OF THE BAG.

TURN THE BAG RIGHT SIDE OUT AND PRESS WELL. TO CLOSE THE BAG, SLIP THE LONG LOOP THROUGH THE SHORT ONE AND PUT YOUR ARM THROUGH IT.

Concerning YOU

Patchwork Quilt

SOME GIRLS LOVE SEWING—OTHERS FIND THAT A LITTLE GOES A LONG WAY! HOW EVER YOU MAY FEEL ABOUT IT, MAKING A PATCHWORK QUILT PLEASES BOTH TASTES. YOU CAN DO AS MUCH, OR AS LITTLE, AS YOU LIKE—AT ANY TIME.

NEARLY EVERYBODY HAS A RAG-BAG FULL OF SCRAPS OF MATERIAL WHICH HAVE BEEN LEFT OVER FROM DRESS-MAKING OR CURTAINS.

SORT OUT YOUR MATERIALS AND CHOOSE THE WASHABLE ONES. IT DOESN'T MATTER WHETHER THE PIECES ARE STRIPED OR SPOTTED, PRINTED OR PLAIN — THE MORE VARIETY THE BETTER.

FRIENDS WILL PROBABLY CONTRIBUTE—AND SWAP PIECES WITH YOU, TOO. MAKING PATCHWORK QUILTS IS A HOBBY THAT'S CATCHING.

DON'T STICK TO ANY PARTICULAR SHAPES IN YOUR MATERIALS. SIMPLY TURN DOWN THE RAW EDGES AND TACK THE PIECES TOGETHER, ONE AT A TIME; THEN HERRING-BONE STITCH THEM ALONG THE FOLDED EDGES, WITH GOOD STRONG THREAD OR EMBROIDERY COTTON.

GRADUALLY YOUR QUILT WILL GROW UNTIL YOU CAN START SHAPING IT, AS YOU GO ALONG, INTO A RECTANGLE OF THE SIZE YOU WANT.

BACK THE FINISHED QUILT WITH A PIECE OF STRONG, PLAIN MATERIAL. YOUR NEW, GAY BED COVER WILL LOOK ATTRACTIVE WITH ANY COLOUR-SCHEME.

Concerning YOU

BEACH-WEAR

HAVING THE RIGHT CLOTHES WITH YOU ON HOLIDAY IS SIMPLY A MATTER FOR CAREFUL PLANNING. MAKE A PACKING-LIST A WEEK BEFORE YOU GO ON HOLIDAY AND ADD THINGS TO IT AS YOU THINK OF THEM.

BE SURE TO TAKE A GAY, ROOMY BEACH-BAG WHICH WILL HOLD YOUR SUN-OIL, GLASSES, BOOKS AND ANY EXTRA CLOTHING YOU NEED FOR THE BEACH.

THE GOLDEN RULE FOR BEACH-WEAR IS THAT IT SHOULD BE EASY TO PUT ON AND TAKE OFF. REMEMBER THAT ON MOST BEACHES, YOU WILL HAVE NO PRIVACY FOR CHANGING.

SEPARATES ARE IDEAL. YOU CAN WEAR YOUR BATHING COSTUME UNDERNEATH AND JUST SHED THE TOP LAYER WHEN YOU SETTLE DOWN IN THE SUN. THE LIGHT IS DIFFERENT BY THE SEA, AND IT MAKES SUBDUED COLOURS LOOK WISHY-WASHY, SO WEAR BOLD, STRIKING COLOURS, OR WEAR A LOT OF WHITE.

LOOKING FRESH AND CLEAN NEEDN'T MEAN LOTS OF IRONING. THERE ARE A NUMBER OF MATERIALS WHICH NEED LITTLE OR NO IRONING, SO BUY YOUR HOLIDAY WEAR WITH THIS PRINCIPLE IN MIND.

REMEMBER THAT THERE IS ALWAYS A BREEZE BY THE SEA, SO WEAR A SKIRT MADE OF A FAIRLY FIRM MATERIAL. FLIMSY CLOTHES CAN MEAN A LOT OF TROUBLE!

A THICK JACKET OR A CARDIGAN IS AN ESSENTIAL FOR EVERY HOLIDAY.

IF POSSIBLE, BUY ONE IN A NEUTRAL SHADE SO THAT YOU CAN WEAR IT OVER ANY OF YOUR CLOTHES. NAVY, WHITE OR BEIGE ARE THE COLOURS WHICH WILL TONE WITH NEARLY EVERYTHING.

Concerning YOU

Presents on a Shoe-String

SOMEBODY'S BIRTHDAY COMING ALONG SOON AND YOU WANT TO GIVE HIM OR HER A PRESENT, BUT MONEY'S SHORT; SO WHAT DO YOU DO? *MAKE* A PRESENT.

HERE'S THE WAY TO MAKE A TIE-HOLDER FOR FATHER, BROTHER OR BOY FRIEND. BEND A YARD LONG PIECE OF WIRE INTO A NARROW V-SHAPE AND CURL THE ENDS WITH PLIERS SO THAT THEY WON'T CATCH IN THE TIE.

YOU THEN GRIP BOTH SIDES OF THE 'V' IN ONE HAND AND SLIP IT INTO THE TIE SO THAT IT RELAXES AND KEEPS IT IN SHAPE

FOR THE TODDLER — A MAT AND BIB SET. CUT A 12" x 20" PIECE OF PLASTIC AND BIND WITH BIAS BINDING. THE BIB IS A PIECE 9" x 12" WITH A HALF-CIRCLE CUT OUT FOR THE NECK. BIND THE BIB, LEAVING LOOSE ENDS FOR TYING ON.

MOTHER WILL LIKE A GAY TABLE-MAT SET THAT'S HEAT-PROOF AND LOOKS PRETTY. COVER SOME ASBESTOS MATS WITH STRIPED COTTON MATERIAL, AND PUT A FRILL ROUND EACH.

FOR YOUR GIRL-FRIEND — A TRIO OF PADDED AND PERFUMED CLOTHES HANGERS. COVER EACH HANGER WITH COTTON-WOOL AND AN ODDMENT OF SILK OR SATIN. COVER HOOKS WITH SCRAPS CUT ON THE CROSS.

FILL TINY HEART-SHAPED CUSHIONS WITH COTTON-WOOL AND LAVENDER. SEW ONE AT EACH END OF HANGERS.

Concerning YOU

Pen Pals

EVERYONE WOULD LIKE TO TRAVEL AND MEET PEOPLE — BUT NOT EVERYONE CAN AFFORD IT. HOWEVER, A GOOD SUBSTITUTE FOR TRAVELLING IS HAVING A PEN-PAL.

BUREAU DE POSTE

HOW DO YOU SET ABOUT GETTING A PEN-PAL? WELL, IF YOU WOULD LIKE TO WRITE TO SOMEONE IN THE BRITISH ISLES, *GIRL* CAN ARRANGE IT — BUT THERE ARE ORGANIZATIONS WHICH CAN PUT YOU IN TOUCH WITH PEOPLE FROM ALMOST EVERY FOREIGN COUNTRY.

IN YOUR FIRST LETTER, TELL YOUR NEW FRIEND ALL ABOUT YOURSELF. WRITE CLEARLY AND NATURALLY — PARTICULARLY IF YOUR PEN-PAL DOESN'T SPEAK MUCH ENGLISH.

IT IS ALWAYS A GOOD PLAN TO EXCHANGE PHOTOGRAPHS, BOTH OF YOURSELF AND OF THE PLACE WHERE YOU LIVE. IT IS MUCH EASIER TO WRITE TO SOMEONE WHEN YOU KNOW WHAT THEY LOOK LIKE!

IF YOU HAVE A FOREIGN PEN-PAL, DO TAKE THE OPPORTUNITY OF WRITING TO HER IN HER OWN LANGUAGE OCCASIONALLY, IF YOU KNOW IT AT ALL.

THIS IS ONLY POLITE, AND IT WILL HELP YOU TO BRUSH-UP YOUR LANGUAGES.

ASK HER TO CORRECT YOUR MISTAKES, AND DO THE SAME FOR HER IF SHE REPLIES IN ENGLISH.

EXCHANGE VISITS ARE OFTEN ARRANGED BETWEEN PEN-PALS, BUT EVEN IF YOU NEVER MEET YOUR PEN-PAL IN THE FLESH, YOU WILL FIND THAT LETTER WRITING CAN GIVE YOU FRIENDS ALL OVER THE WORLD.

Concerning YOU

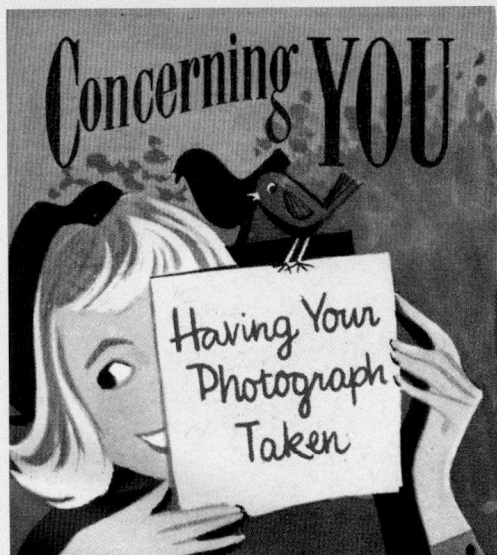

Having Your Photograph Taken

IT'S FUN TO KEEP A PHOTOGRAPHIC RECORD OF YOUR LIFE. PASTING HOLIDAY SNAPS INTO THE ALBUM ON A WINTER'S EVENING BRINGS BACK HAPPY MEMORIES OF SUNNY DAYS.

BUT NOW AND AGAIN — USUALLY AT MOTHER'S REQUEST — YOU MAY FIND YOURSELF VISITING A PROFESSIONAL PHOTOGRAPHER TO HAVE A STUDIO PORTRAIT TAKEN.

VERY OFTEN THE RELAXED CASUALNESS OF SNAPSHOTS IS LOST WHEN THE STUDIO LIGHTS ARE TURNED ON, AND THERE'S A STRAINED LOOK ABOUT THE RESULTING PHOTOGRAPH.

TO FEEL NATURAL AND AT EASE IN FRONT OF THE CAMERA, REMEMBER THAT SIMPLICITY IS ALL IMPORTANT. SO KEEP YOUR NECKLINE PLAIN AND YOUR HAIR ITS USUAL STYLE.

AND HERE'S A TIP THAT HELPS ENORMOUSLY. ASK THE PHOTOGRAPHER IF HE'LL PLACE A MIRROR SOMEWHERE NEAR THE CAMERA.

THEN GIVE *YOURSELF* A BIG SMILE — IT'S MUCH EASIER!

Concerning YOU

Invalid in the House

WHEN MOTHER IS ILL, SHE'S LUCKY IF SHE HAS A DAUGHTER WHO CAN COPE. BESIDES HELPING TO RUN THE HOUSE, THERE ARE THINGS YOU CAN DO TO MAKE LIFE MORE PLEASANT FOR HER.

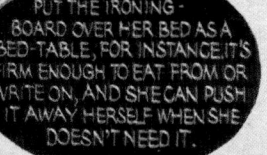

PUT THE IRONING-BOARD OVER HER BED AS A BED-TABLE, FOR INSTANCE; IT'S FIRM ENOUGH TO EAT FROM OR WRITE ON, AND SHE CAN PUSH IT AWAY HERSELF WHEN SHE DOESN'T NEED IT.

IF THERE'S AN ELECTRIC PLUG IN THE BEDROOM YOU CAN DO THE IRONING THERE, TOO. MOTHER WILL WELCOME THE COMPANY IF SHE HAS TO BE ALONE MUCH OF THE TIME.

FIRST THING EVERY MORNING, BRING HER A BOWL OF WARM WATER, TOWEL, SOAP, FACE-FLANNEL, TOOTH-BRUSH AND PASTE, BRUSH AND COMB AND LAVENDER WATER. HAIR DONE, FACE WASHED, TEETH CLEANED, SHE WILL FEEL FAR BETTER.

A FRESH FLOWER FROM THE GARDEN, ON HER BREAKFAST TRAY EACH MORNING, WILL CHEER HER UP, TOO.

ALL THE THINGS AN INVALID NEEDS SHOULD BE WITHIN REACH—FRESH WATER AND A GLASS, MEDICINE, AND SOME FRUIT.

LYING IN BED CAN BE BORING, SO KEEP THE INVALID SUPPLIED WITH MAGAZINES, CHANGE HER LIBRARY BOOK REGULARLY, AND MAKE SURE THAT SHE HAS WRITING MATERIALS AND HER KNITTING!

Concerning YOU
ALL CHANGE

WHEN LIFE GETS INTO A BORING ROUTINE, ONLY YOU CAN CHANGE IT. TRY THESE WAYS OF GETTING OUT OF A RUT.

SWITCH THE FURNITURE AROUND IN YOUR BEDROOM. YOU'LL FIND YOU GET ANOTHER SLANT ON THINGS WHEN YOUR BED'S IN A DIFFERENT POSITION.

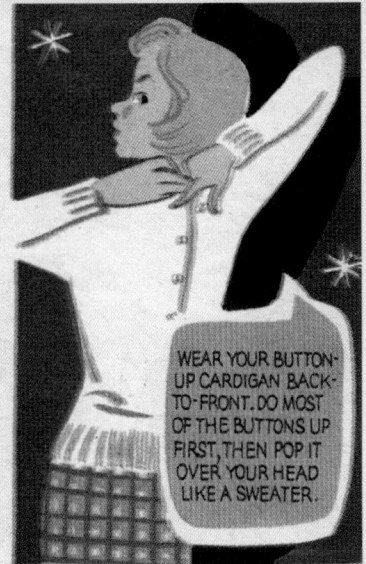

WEAR YOUR BUTTON-UP CARDIGAN BACK-TO-FRONT. DO MOST OF THE BUTTONS UP FIRST, THEN POP IT OVER YOUR HEAD LIKE A SWEATER.

DYE A PAIR OF SHOES A DARKER SHADE—BUT BE CAREFUL TO WEAR RUBBER GLOVES FOR THE JOB.

IF YOU'VE NEVER HAD A COLD BATH BEFORE — TAKE THE PLUNGE AND HAVE ONE NOW. IT'S WONDERFULLY REFRESHING!

CHANGE YOUR HAIR-STYLE: EVEN PARTING YOUR HAIR ON THE OTHER SIDE MAKES YOU LOOK AND FEEL A NEW PERSON.

GO TO YOUR SCHOOL (OR JOB) A DIFFERENT WAY; TAKE YOUR TIME AND ENJOY IT, EVEN IF IT IS A LONGER ROUTE AND MEANS GETTING UP EARLIER.

Concerning YOU

Handy Hints

THERE ARE DOZENS OF SMALL THINGS YOU CAN DO IN THE HOUSE THAT ARE FUN — BESIDES MAKING LIFE EASIER FOR MOTHER.

KNOT TOGETHER THOSE ODD LENGTHS OF STRING THAT AREN'T LONG ENOUGH FOR TYING PARCELS. THEN, USING THICK NEEDLES, KNIT THEM INTO DISH-CLOTHS.

PUT ALL YOUR SPENT MATCHES INTO EMPTY MATCH-BOXES. WHEN FULL, THEY MAKE WONDERFUL FIRE-LIGHTERS.

HAS THE ROLLING-PIN A PROPER HOME IN YOUR KITCHEN?

IT'S EASY TO GIVE IT ONE BY FIXING TWO HOOKS ON THE WALL ABOVE THE WORK-TABLE; THE HOOKS SUPPORT THE HANDLES.

LAST YEAR'S PYJAMAS TOO SHORT? CUT OFF A LITTLE MORE, TRIM WITH BRODERIE ANGLAIS AND YOU HAVE FASHIONABLE SHORTIE PYJAMAS.

WHEN A BATH-TOWEL FINALLY GETS BEYOND NORMAL WEAR, MAKE A 'SHAM-POO-TOWEL'. CUT A HOLE IN THE MIDDLE AND THREAD ELASTIC ROUND IT. SLIPPED OVER YOUR HEAD, IT FITS SNUGLY AND PROTECTS YOU FROM DRIPS AND SPLASHES.

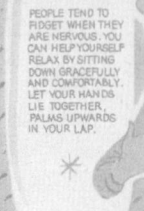